SPEAKING AMERICAN*

***How Y'all, Youse, and You Guys Talk**

A Visual Guide

SPEAKING AMERICAN*

*How Y'all, Youse, and You Guys Talk

A Visual Guide

JOSH KATZ

Houghton Mifflin Harcourt
Boston New York 2016

www.hmhco.com

Library of Congress Cataloging-in-Publication Data is available.
ISBN 978-0-544-70339-1

The maps on pages 4–43, 52–87, 94–119, 127–165, and 173–193 draw on data collected in response to surveys that included questions appearing in the Harvard Dialect Survey, by Bert Vaux and Scott Golder (Harvard University Linguistics Department, 2003), among the topics surveyed. The examples of terms for rain while the sun is shining are drawn from responses compiled in Vaux's 1998 "Sunshower Summary."

All maps courtesy of the author

Book design by Stoltze Design

Printed in China
SCP 10 9 8 7 6 5 4 3 2 1

* To my mom, who always encouraged me to ask questions, and my dad, whose funny accent inspired my curiosity about language.

CONTENTS

AUTHOR'S NOTE AND INTRODUCTION

Drawing on work from the *Dictionary of American Regional English,* the Harvard Dialect Survey, and suggestions from friends and family, in the fall of 2013 I set out to develop an online survey to gather data on how Americans talk. The maps that follow are a product of that survey—which collected more than 350,000 unique responses. Enjoy.

1

Part One

HOW WE LIVE

WHAT WE CALL

THE SHOES WE WEAR TO THE GYM

It used to be that if you wanted something to wear on your feet, your only option was expensive handcrafted leather. But in the late nineteenth century, the assembly-line efficiency of the Industrial Revolution and the advent of new materials like vulcanized rubber gave rise to new, cheap, mass-produced footwear. Typically, it had canvas uppers and soft rubber soles.

What to call this newfangled footwear? People quickly began using them to play tennis, so why not *tennis shoes*? Makes sense. That was good enough for most of the country, but in Boston, for reasons lost to history, people thought: *Hey, I can really sneak around in these things; let's call them* sneakers. And from the shoes' rubber, or gum, soles, we also got the word *gumshoe,* which didn't take hold as a name for the shoe but came to be associated with skulking about. Now it's common slang for a detective.

As with many of the words in this book, no one can quite agree on who invented the term *sneakers* first, but it's been around since at least 1887, when the *Boston Journal of Education* wryly observed, "It is only the harassed schoolmaster who can fully appreciate the pertinency of the name." A few years later, an ad for the Boston-based department store Jordan Marsh was published, hawking its *sneakers* for 50 cents a pop. By the early twentieth century, *sneakers* had gone mainstream.

Perhaps surprisingly, given the word's dominance in popular media, the common use of *sneakers* fades rapidly today once you're outside the Northeast. What's more, *tennis shoes* shows no sign of abating, with teenagers using the word just as often as those in their sixties and older.

Other popular names include *gym shoes* (Chicago and Cincinnati), *running shoes* (parts of California), or just plain old *shoes* (Hawaii).

CHICAGO and **CINCINNATI** are the two places where majorities would instead don *gym shoes*.

Out in the mountains between **PHILADELPHIA** and **PITTSBURGH**, *sneakers* suddenly gives way to *tennis shoes*.

ATLANTA and **RALEIGH**, while still firmly in *tennis shoes* territory, are more partial to *sneakers* than the surrounding region. This dynamic is common, with many urban centers showing slightly different language patterns than their exurbs.

WHAT WE CALL

A SALE OF ASSORTED HOUSEHOLD ITEMS

Most of the country is split between *garage sale* and *yard sale*, with *garage sale* reaching its peak out in **OKLAHOMA** and **KANSAS** and *yard sale* peaking in eastern **NEW ENGLAND** and **NORTH CAROLINA**.

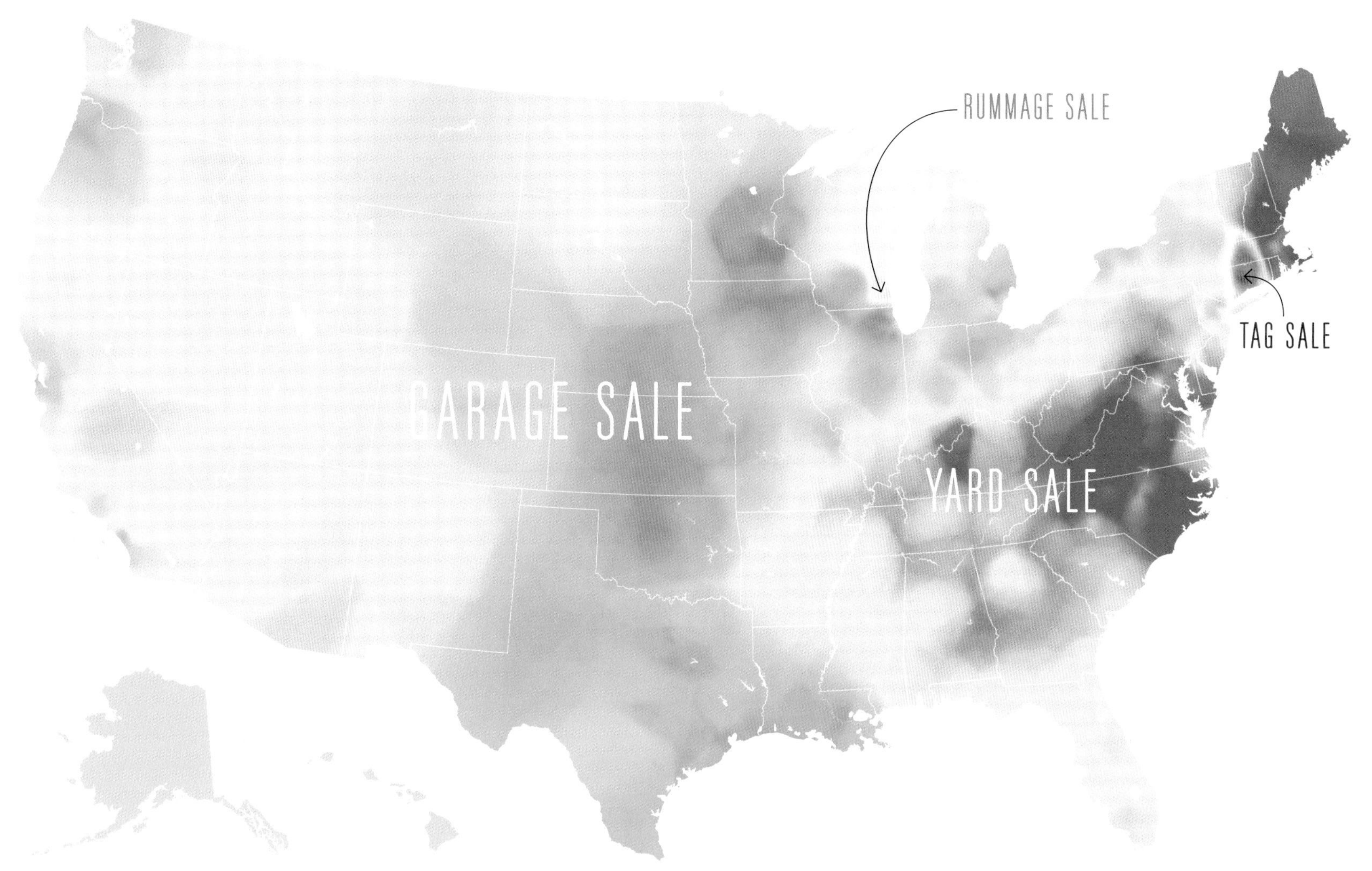

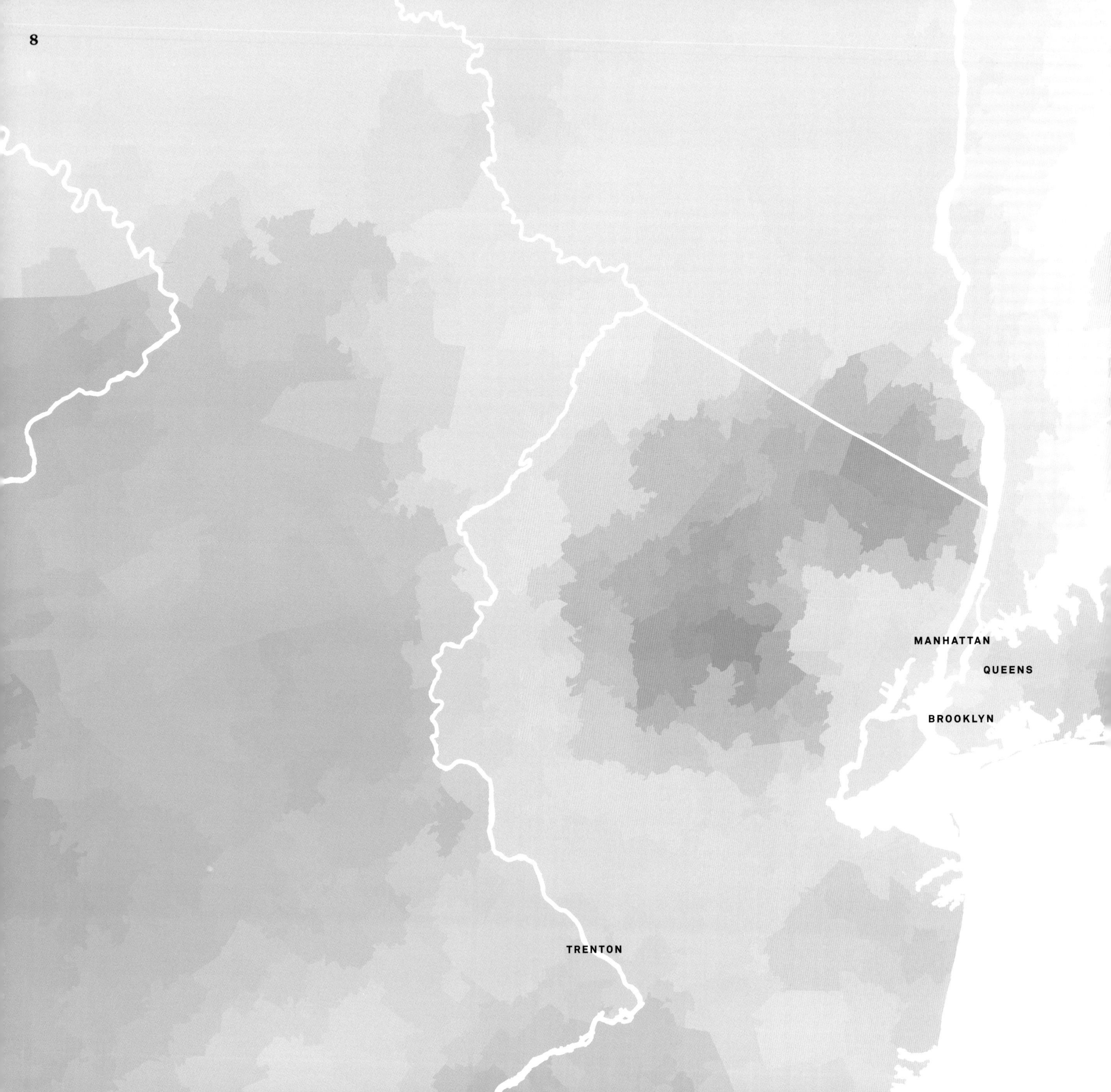
MANHATTAN
QUEENS
BROOKLYN
TRENTON

The *tag sale* is unique to **CONNECTICUT** and western **MASSACHUSETTS**.

The **NEW YORK TRI-STATE AREA** changes from *tag sales* in **CONNECTICUT** to *garage sales* in **NORTH JERSEY** to *yard sales* in **SOUTH JERSEY** and **PHILADELPHIA**.

As you drive along the turnpike into **SOUTH JERSEY**, *garage sales* transition abruptly into *yard sales*.

HARTFORD

NEW HAVEN

TAG SALE: WELCOME TO CONNECTICUT

The *tag sale* is unique to Connecticut and western Massachusetts. It's almost never encountered west of the Hudson and is rarely heard within New York City. It's one of the few dialectology tidbits that Connecticut can call its own—not from wider New England and not from New York.

The origin of the term is fairly straightforward. "You aren't selling your garage, are you?" as one commentator put it during an online debate over language use. "You aren't selling your yard. It's a tag sale. You sell the things that are tagged." To which someone might reply that you aren't selling the tags either, but as a general rule, it's best to avoid wading into the comments.

While Merriam-Webster says the first known use of *tag sale* occurred in 1929, an earlier sense of *tag sale* developed around the beginning of the twentieth century. At that time, a *tag sale* was a specific kind of fundraising effort in which your donation came in the purchase of a tag to show that you'd donated.

PERCENT SAYING *TAG SALE*

0 10 20 30 40 >50%

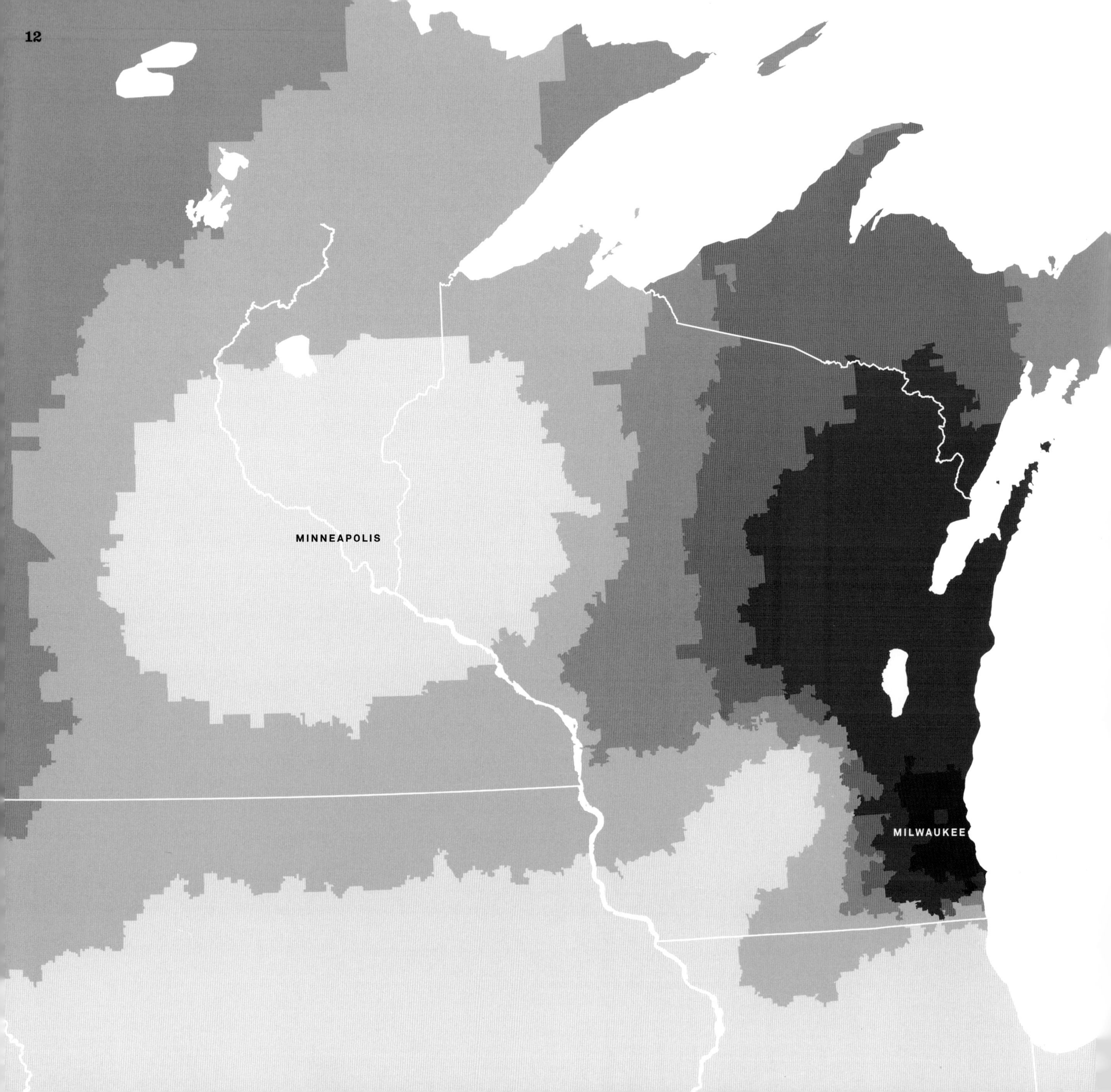
MINNEAPOLIS
MILWAUKEE

RUMMAGE SALE

The residents of southeast Wisconsin see the whole *yard sale* vs. *garage sale* dispute as a moot point. To them, the event is most certainly a *rummage sale*. Which seems like poor branding: *rummage sale* can evoke a big pile of junk and might just sound to a non-Wisconsinite like a random-stuff-I-found-in-my-attic sale. But it works for Wisconsin.

The term can be traced all the way back to the sixteenth century, when *rummage* entered English from the French *arrumage,* meaning arrangement of cargo. The word originally referred specifically to arranging cargo on a ship, hence the term *rummage sale* cropped up in the early 1800s to mean a sale of unclaimed goods at the docks.

PERCENT SAYING *RUMMAGE SALE*

0 10 20 30 40 >50%

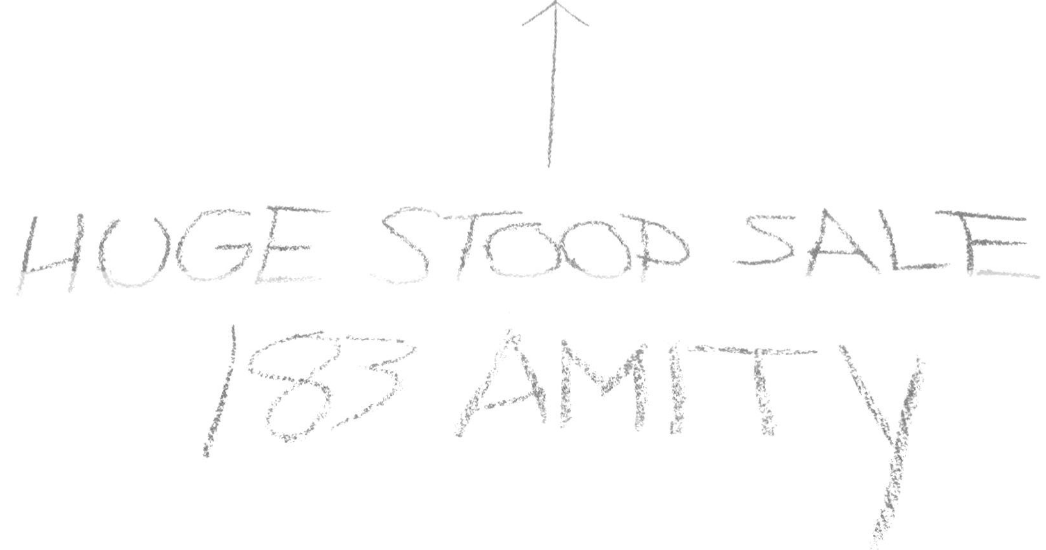

STOOP SALE:
THE HISTORY OF A NEW YORK INSTITUTION

New York has much to offer: world-class food, art, and nightlife, but when it comes to front yards, not so much. Nor, for that matter, are garages commonly encountered in a city where space is at a premium and a second bedroom is a luxury item. But New York does have an abundance of stoops—those staircases leading up from the street to the entrances of row houses and brownstones.

In the eighteenth century, the influence of the Dutch over their former colony remained strong, and the Dutch word *stoep*—meaning a flight of stairs, though also used in the sense of a small porch with seats or benches—had entered the American lexicon as *stoop* by 1755.

Some argue that the ubiquity of stoops in New York is itself a byproduct of the Dutch proclivity for building elevated houses; others, that the stoop functioned to separate the formal entryway to the home from the entrance to the kitchen and other service offices, which were usually kept just below street level.

Regardless, the stoop plays a central role in city life—it is a meeting place, an observation deck, a buffer between the home and the commotion of the streets. And it provides prime real estate for the aptly named *stoop sale,* a term confined almost entirely to New York City.

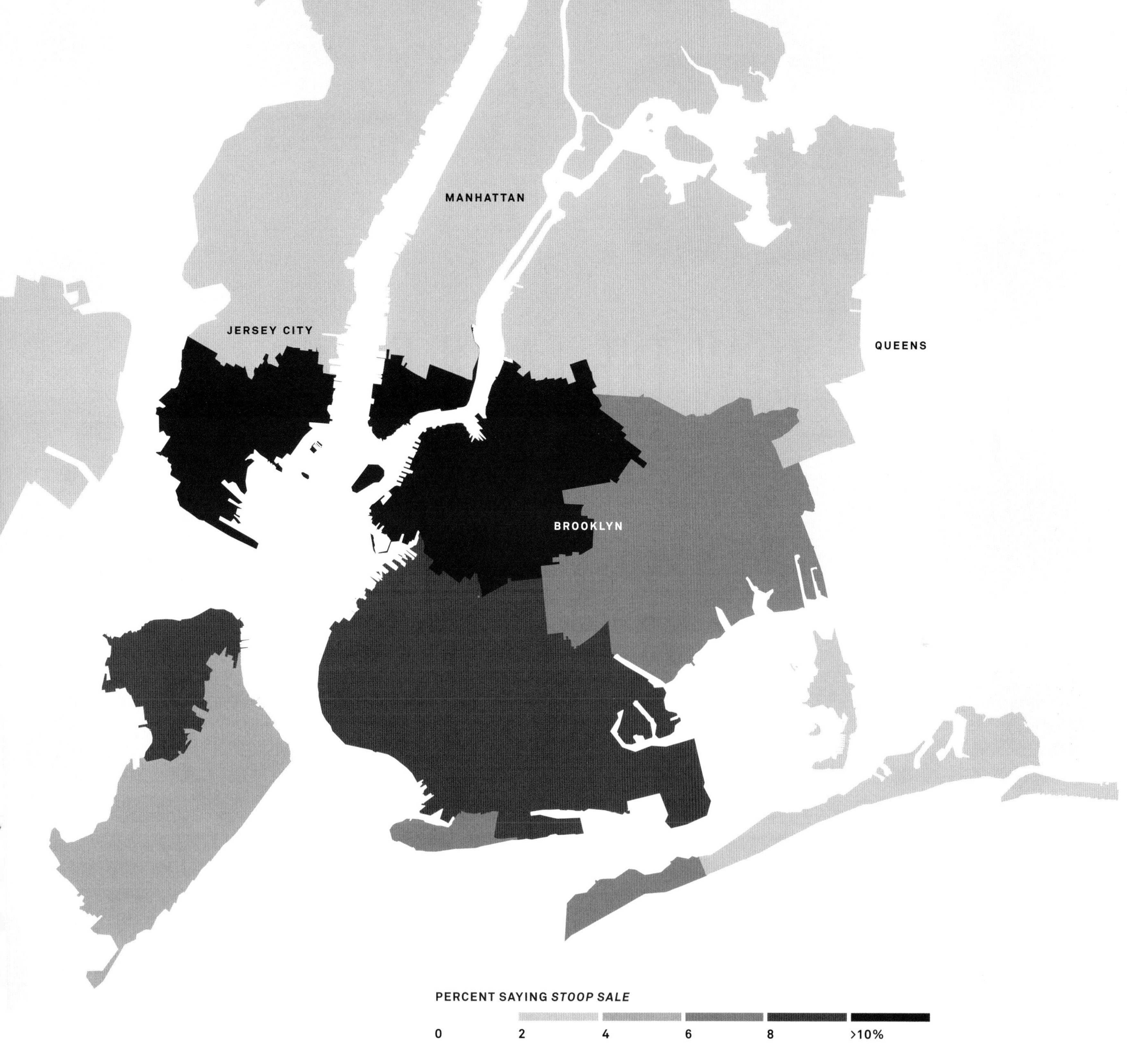
MANHATTAN
JERSEY CITY
QUEENS
BROOKLYN
PERCENT SAYING STOOP SALE
0
2
4
6
8
>10%

AMERICANS ARE DIVIDED OVER LAWN CARE

PERCENT SAYING

0 10 20 30 40 50 75%

MOW THE LAWN 70%

CUT THE GRASS 20%

MOW THE GRASS 9%

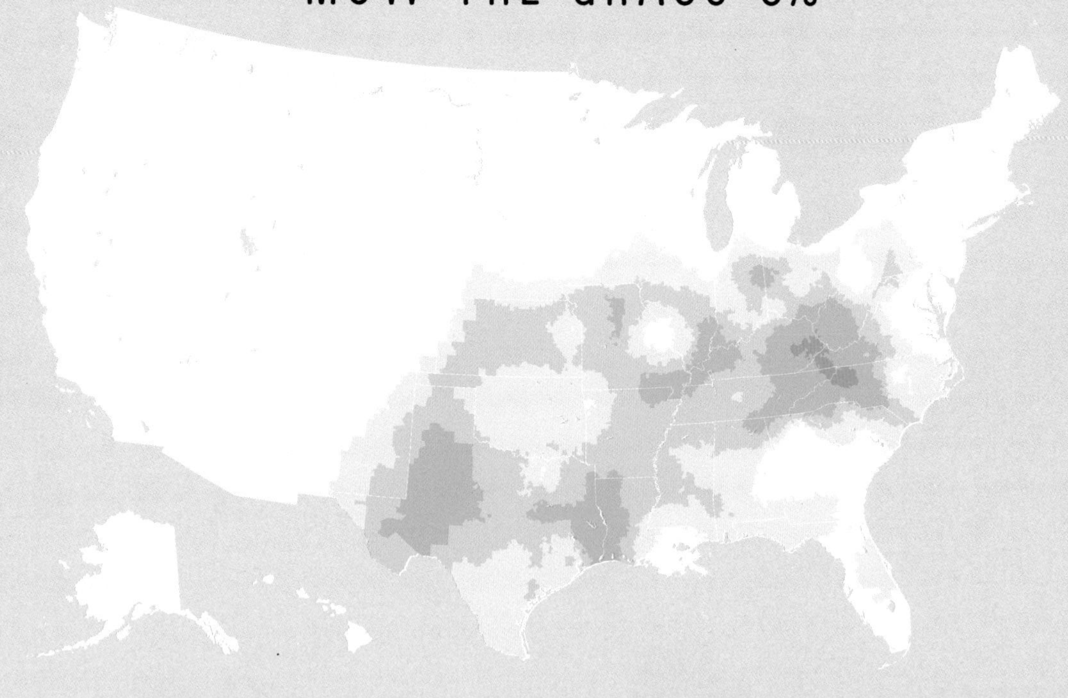

OUT OF THE FRYING PAN, INTO THE SKILLET

Almost three-quarters of people from **LITTLE ROCK, ARKANSAS**, say *skillet*—the highest concentration in the country. With 73 percent of its residents using *skillet,* it's the place you're most likely to hear it, while only 10 percent of people in and around **NEW YORK** and **NORTH JERSEY** use the term.

SKILLET

WHAT WE CALL

PAPER THAT HAS ALREADY BEEN WRITTEN ON

The residents of **DES MOINES** are champions of fine semantic distinctions. Nearly 40 percent of them contend that *scrap paper* be reserved for paper that's no longer usable, while *scratch paper* can still be used for, say, note-taking or solving a tricky math problem. (As an aside, the proper demonym for Des Moines remains, as of this writing, an unsettled question: Des Moinesians? Des Moinesers? Des Moineserians? The world wants to know.)

SCRATCH PAPER

WHERE WE THROW OUR TRASH

Since the 1950s, *trash can* has become increasingly common in American speech. Two in three people born in the 1990s would say *trash can* over *garbage can*.

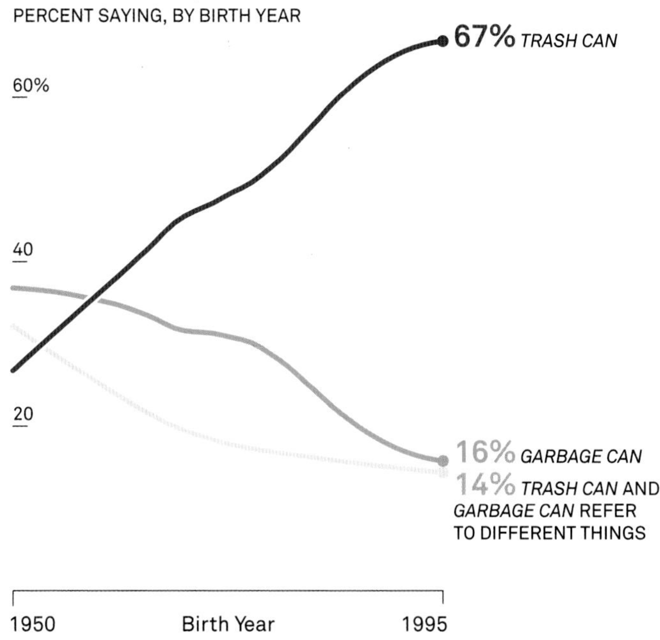

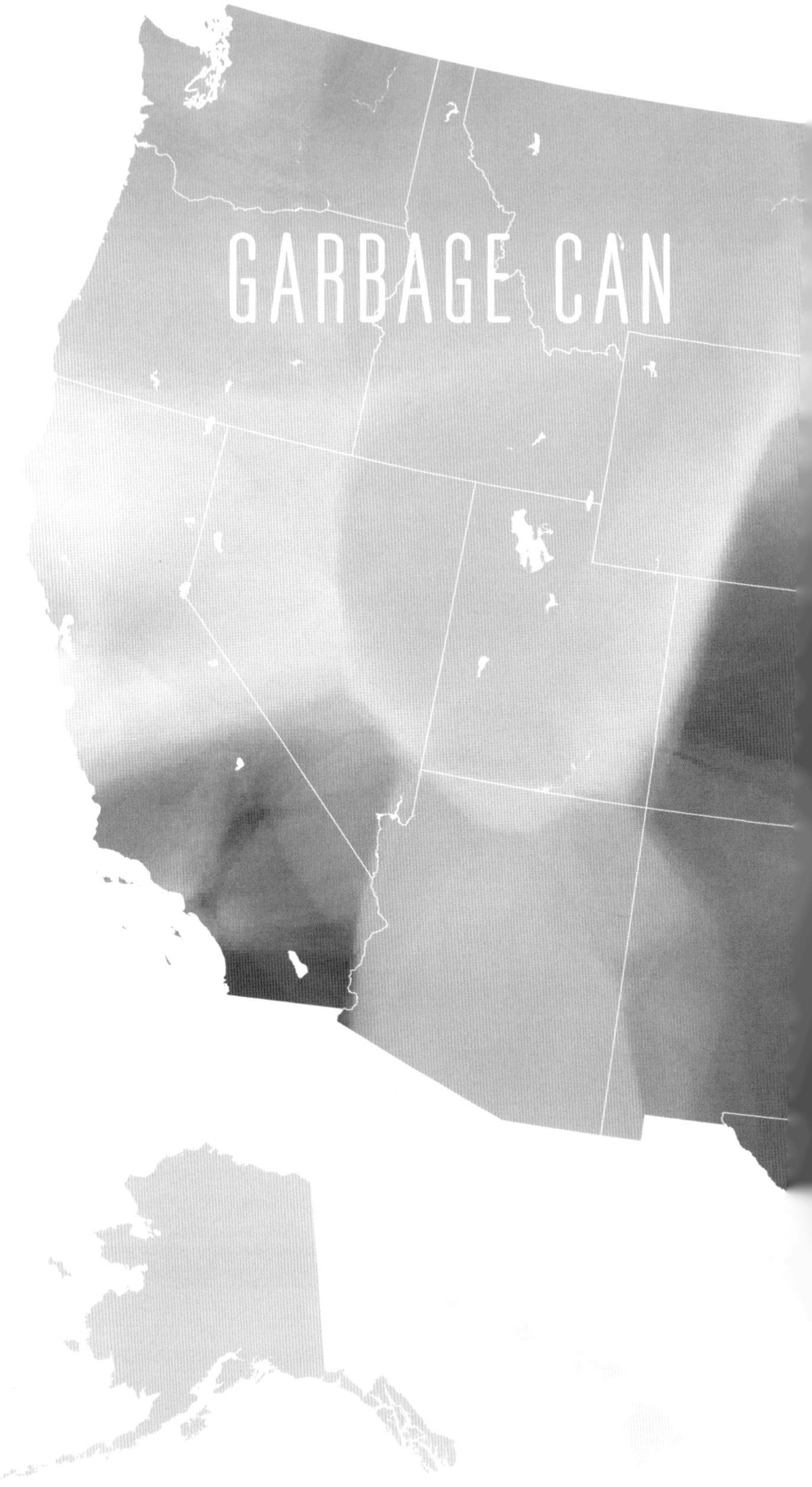

GARBAGE CAN

TRASH CAN

BLESS YOU 73%

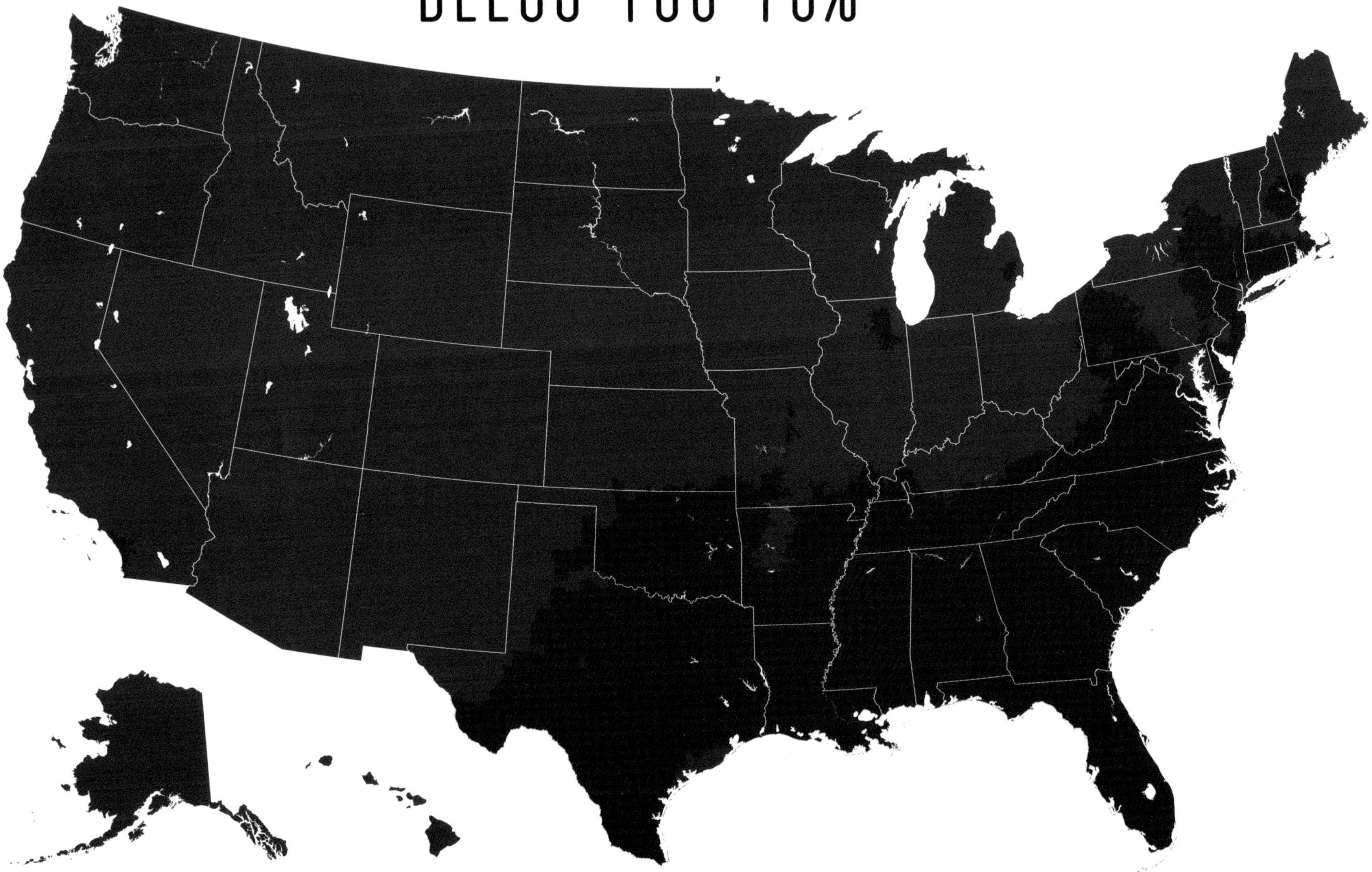

PERCENT SAYING

GESUNDHEIT 18%

A QUESTION OF ETIQUETTE

NOTHING 6%

The practice of offering a comment after a sneeze is almost universal. It extends across a wide range of cultures and languages, from Hindi to Czech to Hebrew. In the Western world, it appears in ancient writings as far back as A.D. 77.

The adoption of the German *gesundheit* (health) began in the early twentieth century amidst an influx of German- and Yiddish-speaking immigrants. It became especially common in Wisconsin and Minnesota, home to large German populations. But its popularity has waned over time—you're now far more likely to hear some variation of *bless you,* even in the upper Midwest.

The post-sneeze remark is also one of the few areas of terminology where gender differences exist, with men slightly more likely to say *gesundheit* than women—and more than twice as likely to say nothing at all.

THE DIVIDING LINE BETWEEN NORTH AND SOUTH

YOU GUYS
Y'ALL
Almost 30 percent of people in **PITTSBURGH** and its surroundings would say *yins*.
In **KENTUCKY** it's *you all*.

Nineteenth-century migration in the United States was primarily a tale of westward expansion. As settlers moved west, they carried their culture—and their language—with them. Thus the divisions seen on the East Coast perpetuated themselves westward, as people from different parts of the East moved to different parts of the West. A linguistic fault line runs from Texas up through Arkansas, then tracks the Ohio River along the northern border of Kentucky toward the Mason-Dixon Line.

One of the clearest expressions of this fault line is the boundary between where they say *you guys* and where they say *y'all*.

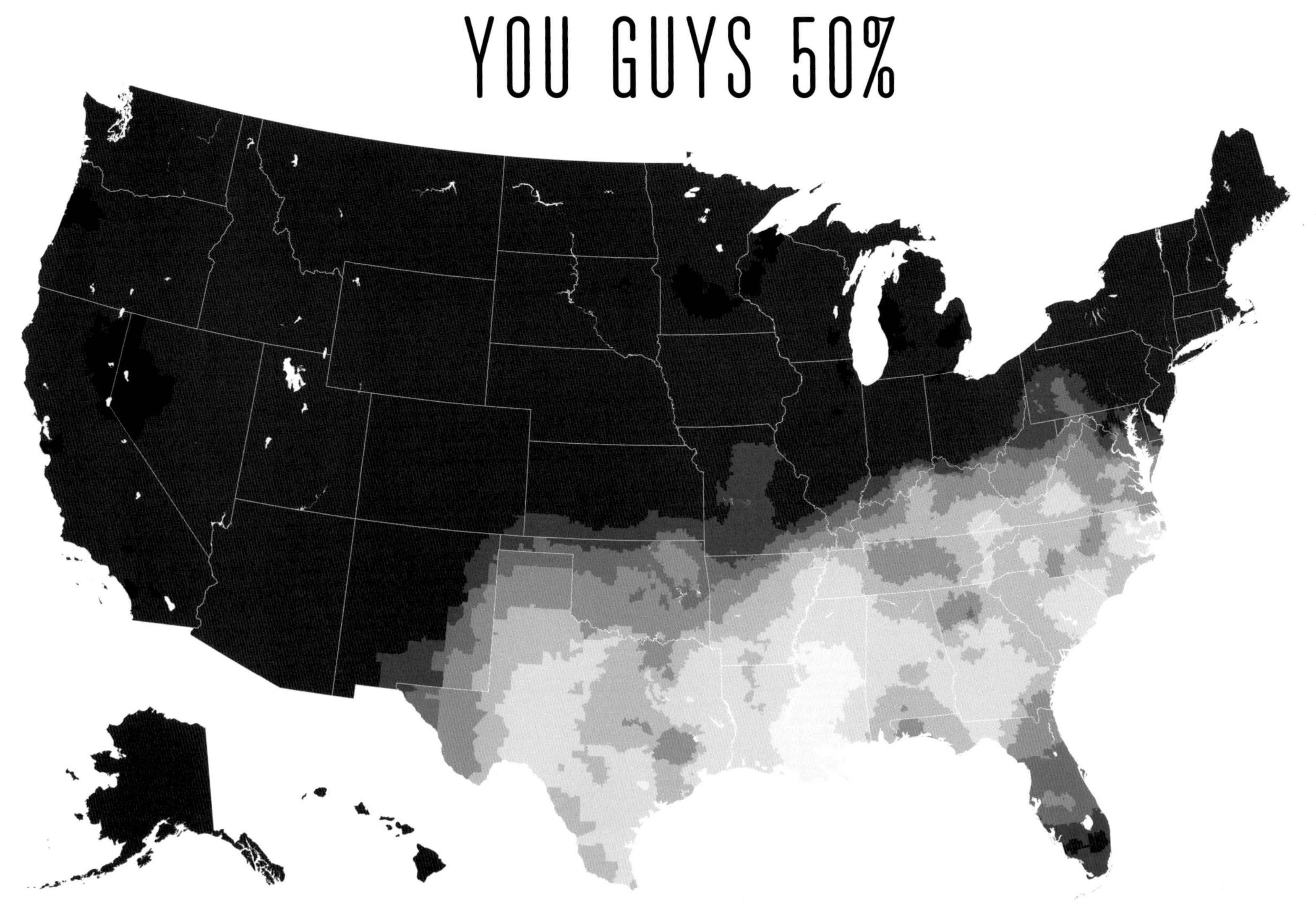

YOU ALL 10%

YOU 10%

YINS <1%

PERCENT SAYING

0 10 20 30 40 50 75%

YOUS/YOUSE

PERCENT SAYING

0 5 10 15 20 >25%

YINS

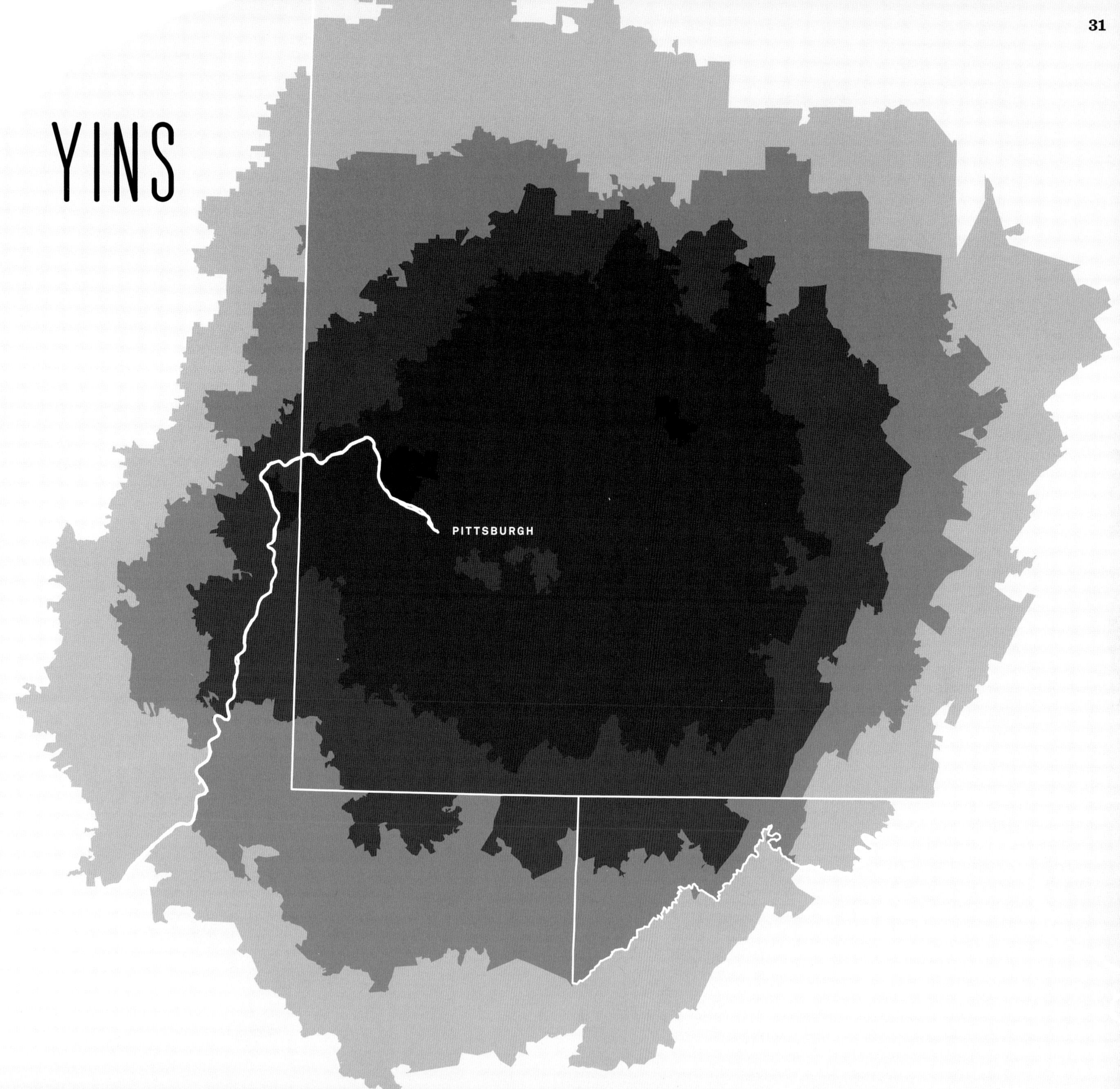

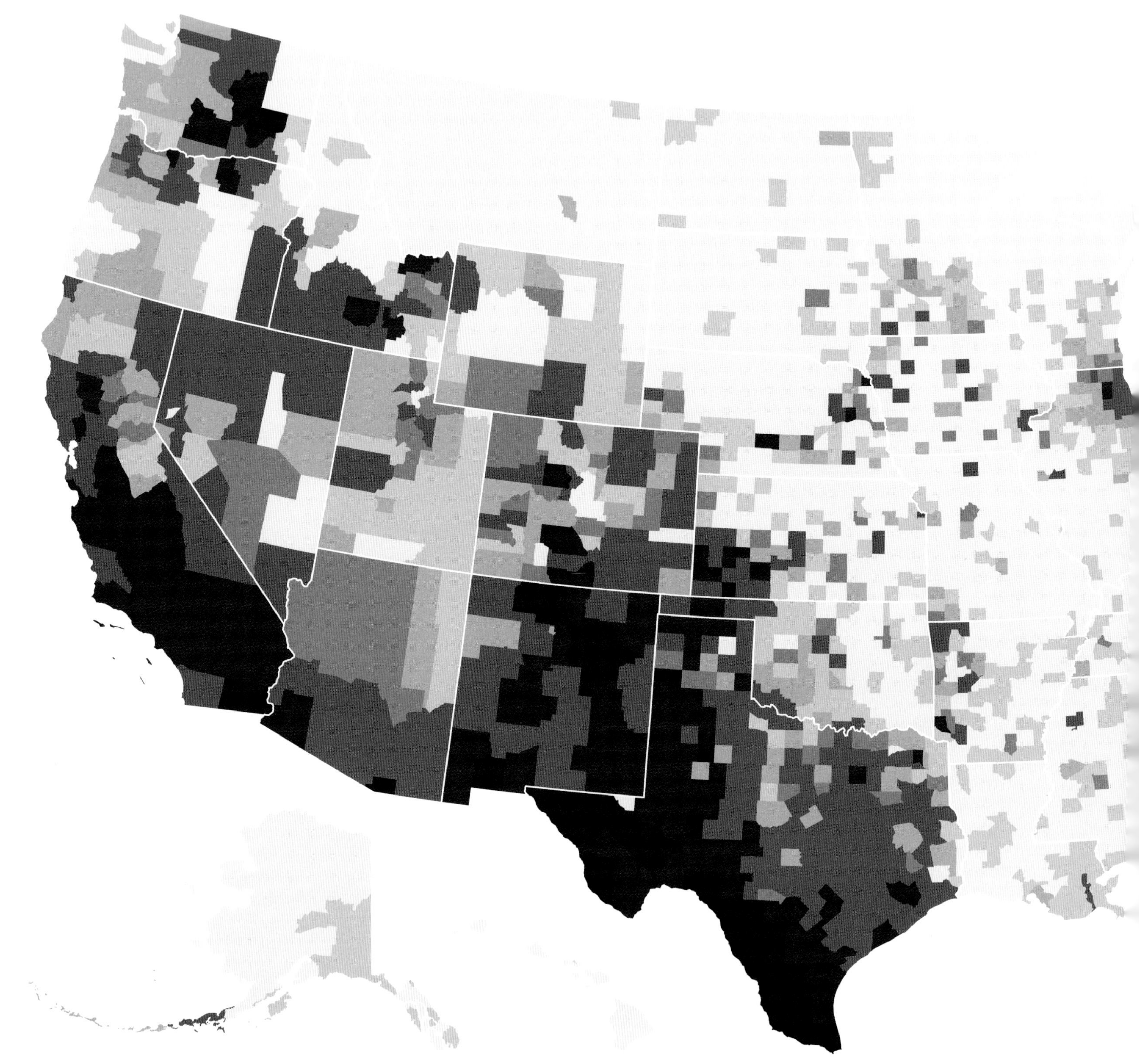

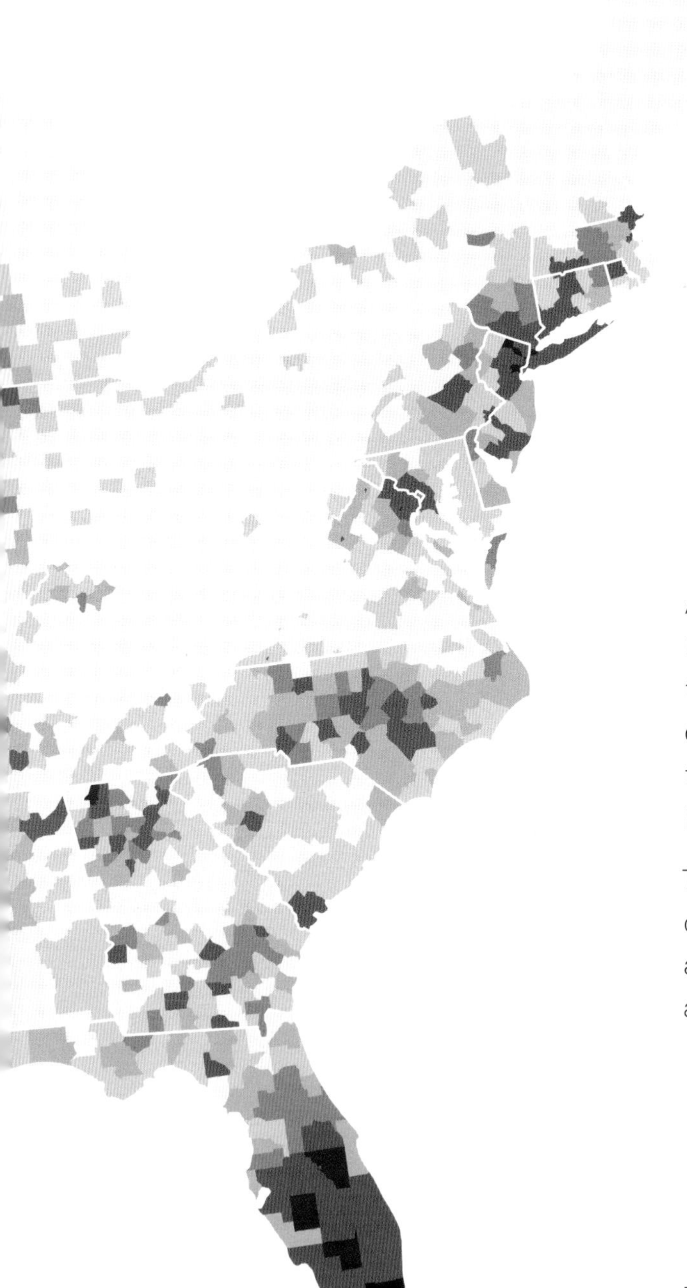

SPEAKING AMERICAN DOESN'T ALWAYS MEAN SPEAKING ENGLISH

Although this book focuses on the many ways of speaking English in America, it would be incomplete without noting that to speak American is not necessarily to speak English. By last count, more than 60 million Americans speak a language other than English in their homes. For more than half of these homes, the language is Spanish.

The distribution of Spanish speakers is of course a function of geography. There are many counties in the Southwest where a majority of households speak Spanish. In Starr County, Texas, a whopping 94 percent of people speak Spanish at home.

HOW WOULD YOU SAY 3:45?

THREE FORTY-FIVE 51%

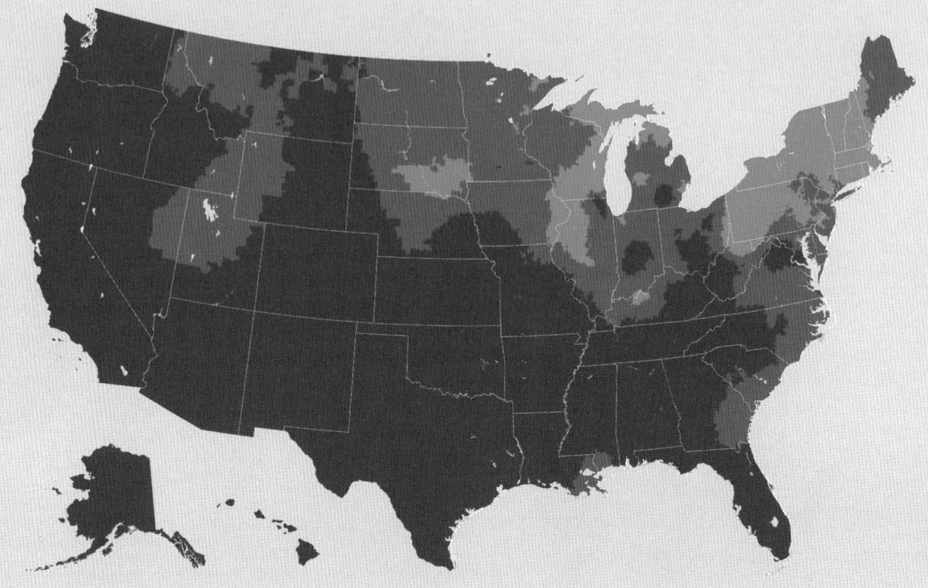

QUARTER TO FOUR 34%

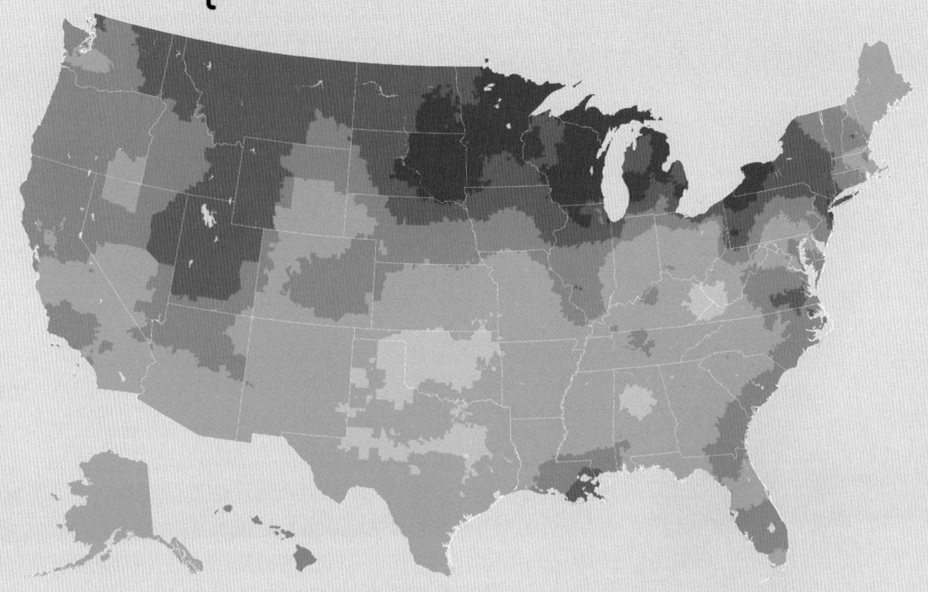

QUARTER TILL FOUR 8%

QUARTER OF FOUR 6%

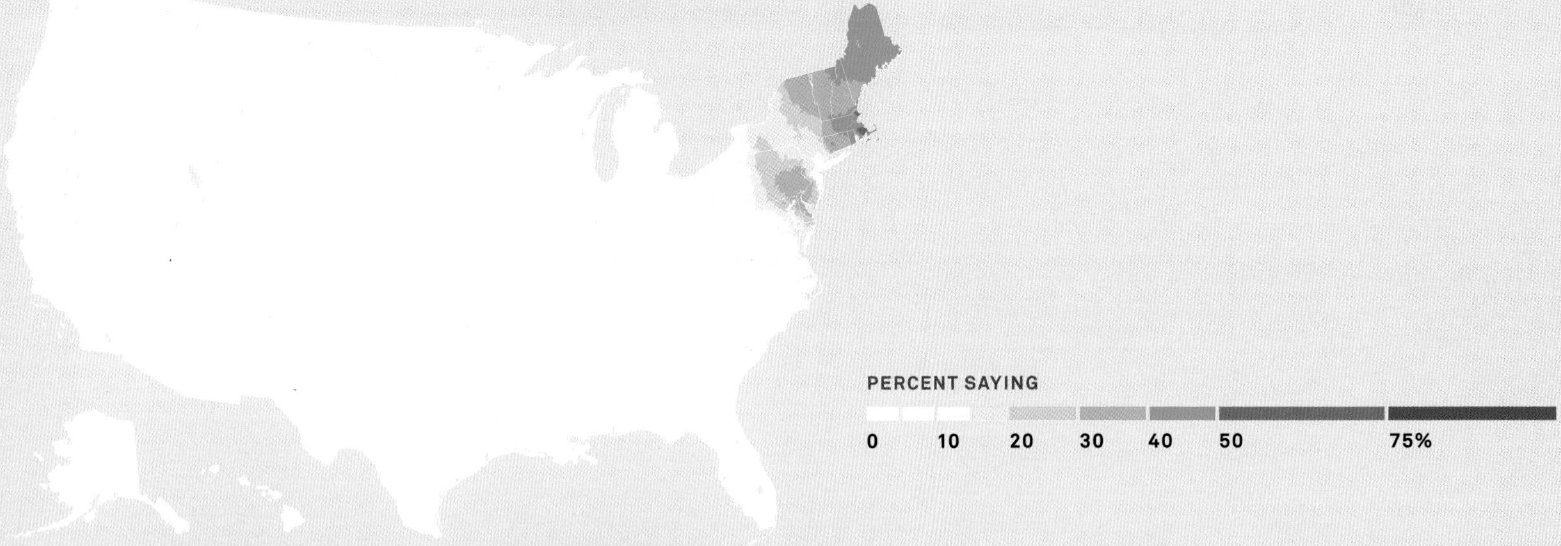

PERCENT SAYING

0 10 20 30 40 50 75%

WHAT WE CELEBRATE

ON THE NIGHT BEFORE HALLOWEEN

From its earliest beginnings, stemming from the Celtic festival of Samhain, Halloween has been associated with mischief.

Lisa Morton, a historian of Halloween, writes that in the 1920s, mischief began to take on a more sinister quality, as arson and vandalism joined more innocent pranks like rapping on neighbors' windows, jamming doorbells, or occassionally tipping over an outhouse. As Halloween became more popular after World War II and developed into a full-fledged national holiday, civil society made a concerted effort to avoid the darker parts of the holiday. They emphasized costume parties, parades, and contests for the best costumes and window decorations.

Around this time, trick-or-treat began to spread throughout the country. It was a way of acknowledging the destructive potential of the festival and, in the process, sublimating it. The efforts worked. In the 1950s and '60s, Halloween was transformed from a destructive night of anarchic vandalism into a night that was, writes historian Nicholas Rogers, "consumer-oriented and infantile" and "a boon for food manufacturers and retailers." By the 1960s, Halloween in the United States had been largely tamed.

But the reformers did not eliminate the pranking. Some of it remained, and other parts of it moved to the night before—October 30, which acquired one of several different names, depending on geography: *Devil's Night* in Michigan and Pittsburgh, *Mischief Night* in South Jersey and Philadelphia, or *Goosey Night* in a tiny sliver of North Jersey. Just as trick-or-treat was turning Halloween into a family-friendly night of consumption, the first written references to the night before Halloween as a night of vandalism and pranking began to emerge.

MISCHIEF NIGHT 8%

DEVIL'S NIGHT 7%

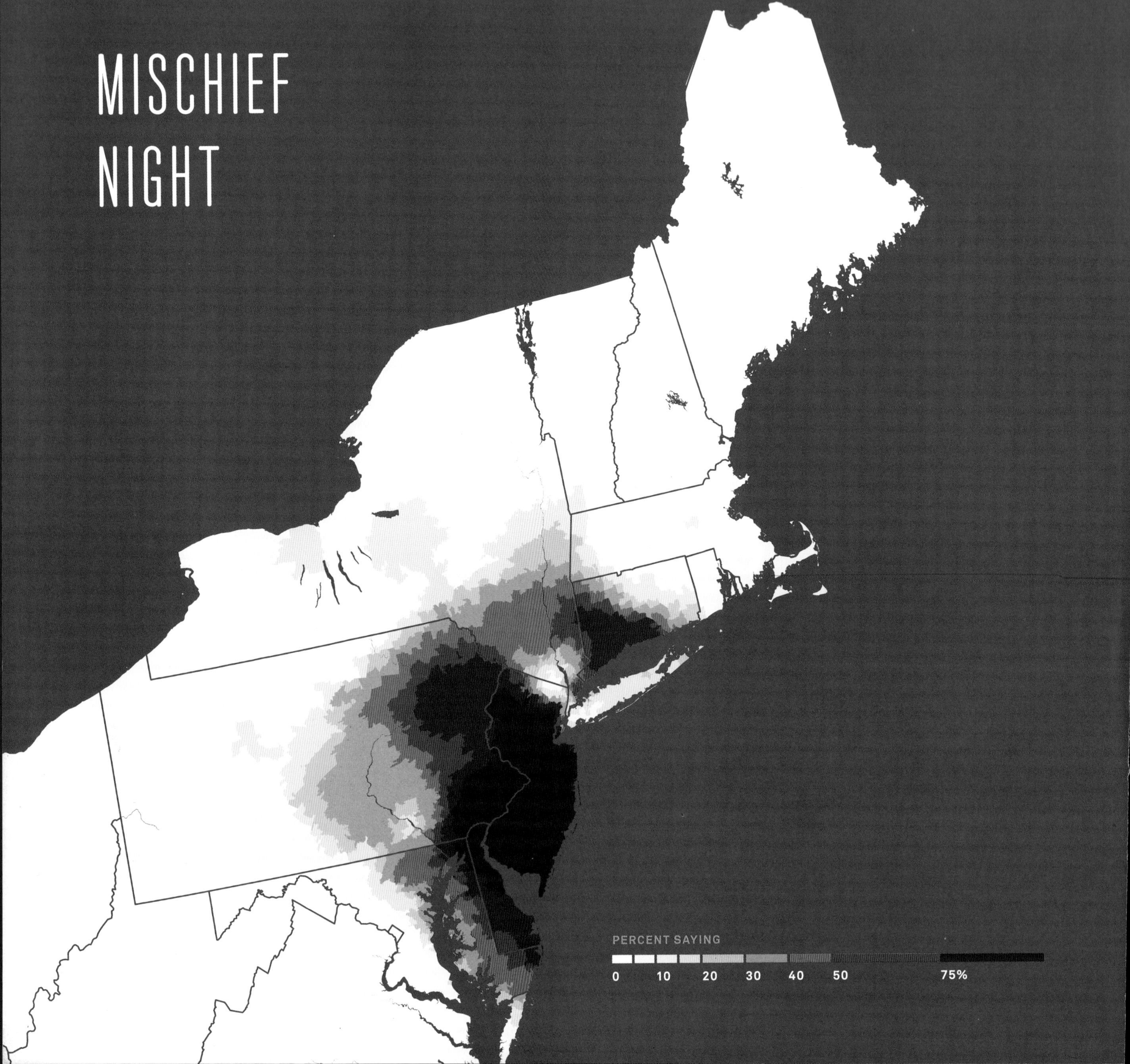
MISCHIEF NIGHT
PERCENT SAYING
0
10
20
30
40
50
75%

GATE NIGHT

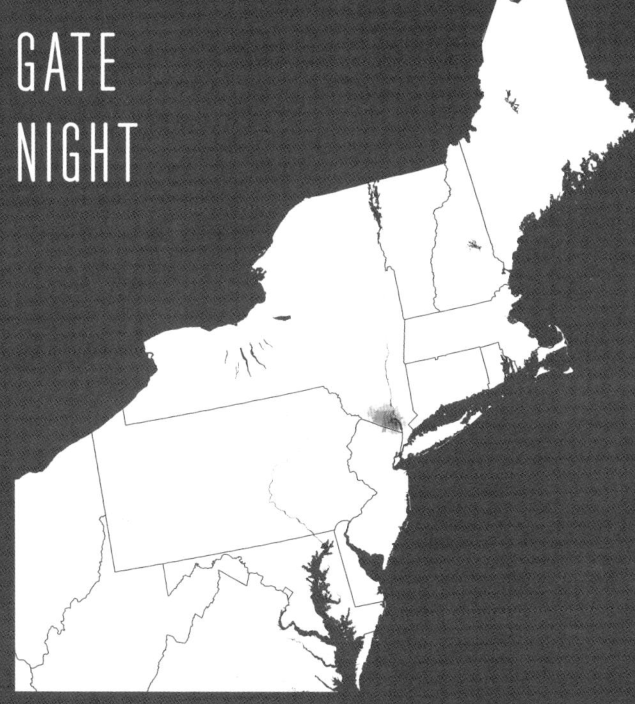

This name can be traced back to the practice of dismantling the gates of nearby houses, removing them from their hinges (and sometimes placing them in the middle of the town square or up in a tree).

CABBAGE NIGHT

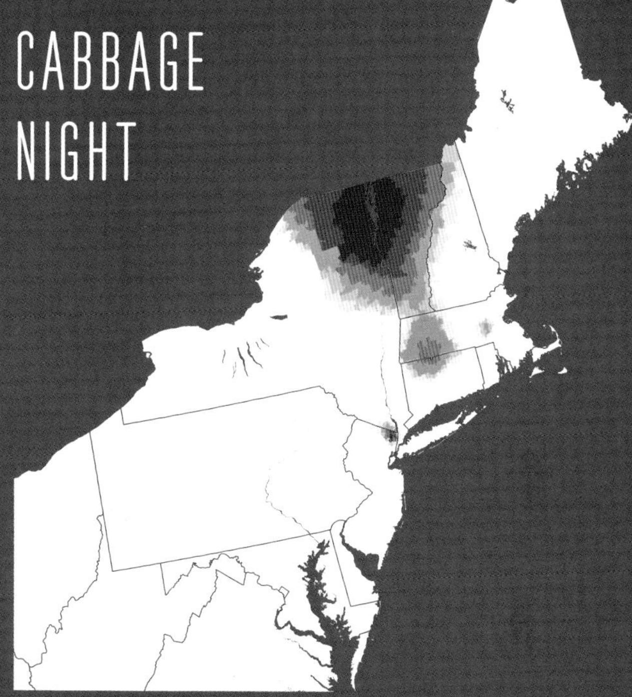

On both the **NEW YORK** and **VERMONT** sides of Lake Champlain, the holiday is often called *Cabbage Night*, a reference to the tradition of raiding nearby cabbage patches, uprooting the vegetables, and hurling them at neighbors' front doors.

GOOSEY NIGHT

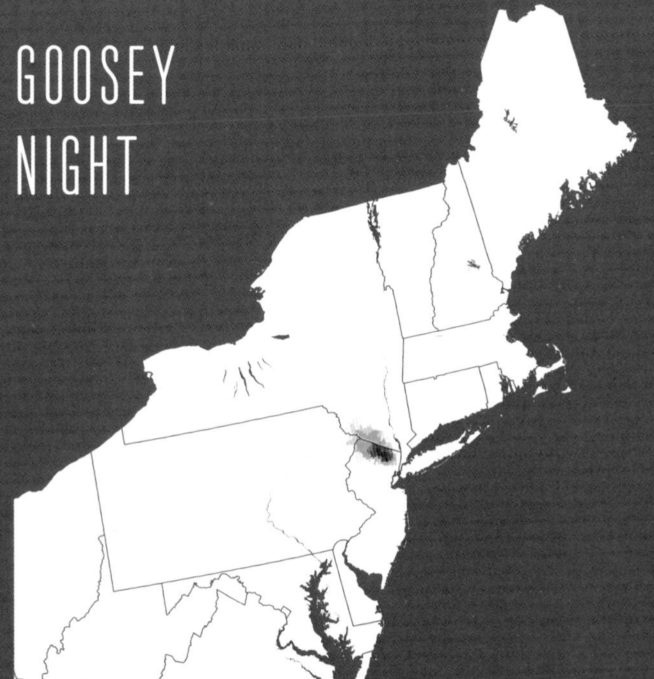

DEVIL'S NIGHT

PROBABLY EASIER
TO JUST POINT
ACROSS THE STREET

About 80 percent of the country would describe something across the street from them diagonally as either *kitty-corner* or *catty-corner,* with the dividing line between the two running east to west across the United States.

Around 93 percent of people from **GREEN BAY**, **WISCONSIN**, say *kitty-corner.*

In scattered sections in and around **NEW YORK CITY** (and also in southern **FLORIDA**), people find both *kitty-corner* and *catty-corner* to be bizarre, so they just say *diagonal*.

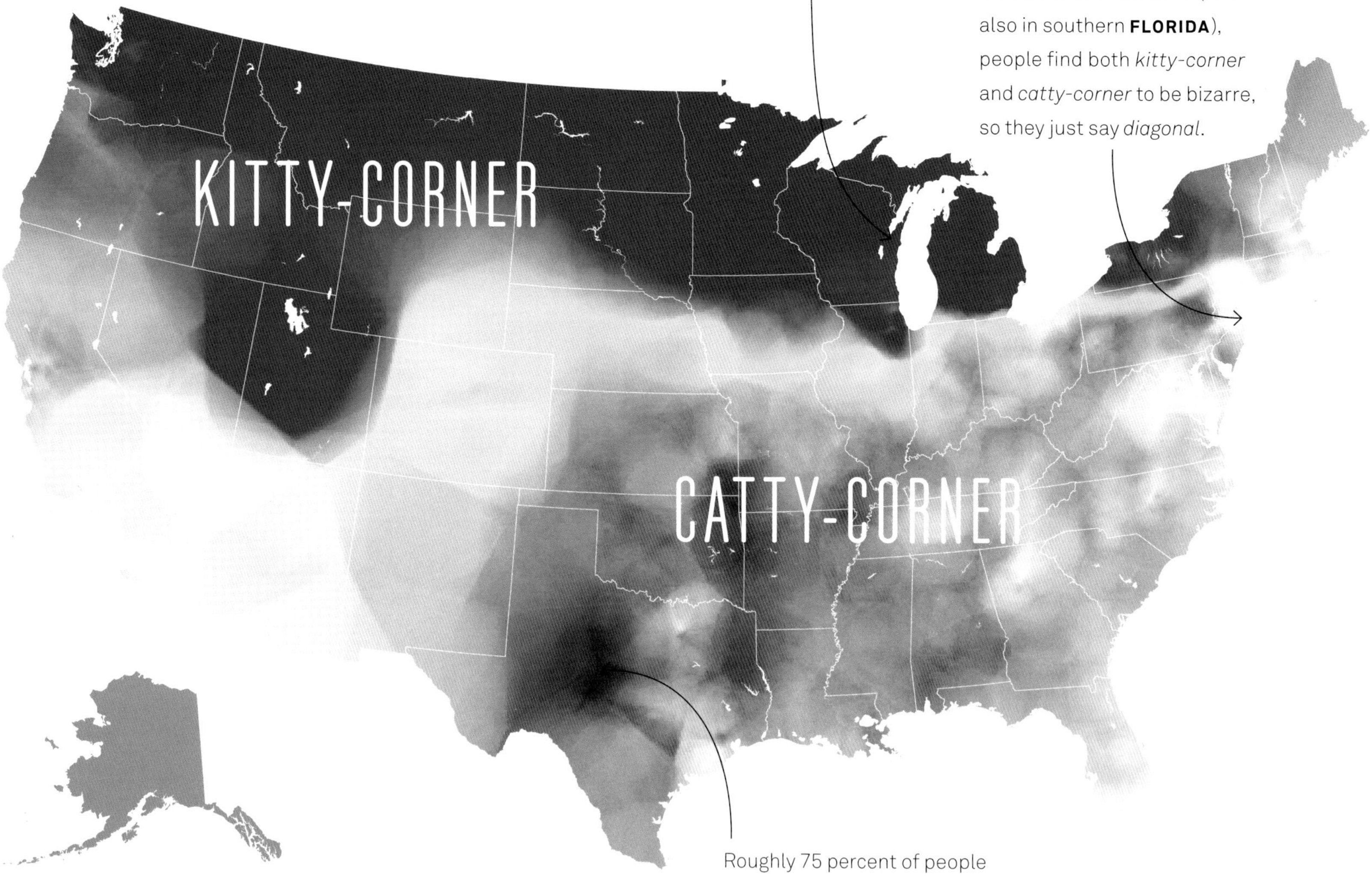

KITTY-CORNER

CATTY-CORNER

Roughly 75 percent of people from central **TEXAS** say *catty-corner.*

HOW TO PRETEND YOU'RE FROM

OHIO

From the outside, Ohio might seem like the kind of state that would have a generic sort of Midwestern dialect, but in reality it's composed of several distinct speech regions, divided between Cleveland in the northeast and Cincinnati in the southwest.

In Cincinnati, 60 percent of people say *gym shoes,* but few call them that in Cleveland, where it's almost always either *tennis shoes* (68 percent) or *sneakers* (28 percent). In Cincinnati, more than 80 percent of people call a woodlouse a *pillbug* or a *roly-poly;* in Cleveland, you're more likely to hear *potato bug*. Cleveland has the *freeway;* Cincinnati, the *expressway*. Cincinnati has *roundabouts*. Cleveland has *traffic circles*.

In Cleveland, on the southern shore of Lake Erie, the strip between the sidewalk and the road is the *tree lawn,* or, elsewhere, the *berm*.

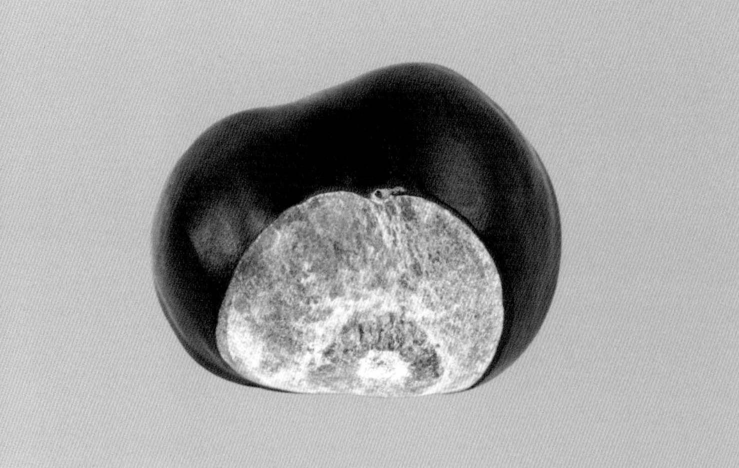

HOW TO PRETEND YOU'RE FROM

WISCONSIN

If you're from Wi-*scon*-sin (not Wis-*con*-sin, as the outsiders would say), throw some *pop* into a *bag* (pronounced *bayg*) and head over to the *covered-dish* (potluck). Bring some *bars* along for dessert and remember to turn left at the *stop-and-go light*.

Here, a water fountain is a *bubbler,* the strip of grass between the sidewalk and the road is the *terrace,* and, as we've seen, it's neither a *garage sale* nor a *yard sale,* but a *rummage sale*.

As for those cheeseheads, as recently as thirty years ago the term was considered an insult ("a stupid, lazy person" in the 1985 edition of the *Dictionary of American Regional English*). But that was before Milwaukee resident Ralph Bruno created the first cheesehead hat in 1987, as Joseph Kapler Jr. reported in the *Wisconsin Magazine of History:* "'I just wanted to take something negative and turn it into a positive,' Bruno [said]. 'The cheesehead was a way to show my pride in Wisconsin and at the same time have fun with an insult.'"

When the hat found its way onto the heads of Green Bay Packers fans—and the Packers found their way back onto the national stage in the 1990s—the term quickly wormed its way into the American consciousness. By the late 1990s, *cheesehead* had become just another word for a Wisconsinite.

HOW TO PRETEND YOU'RE FROM

NEBRASKA

The Cornhusker State is a place where spinning your car in circles is *doing cookies, creek* often sounds like *crik,* and you'd carry your *pop* home in a *sack*. The grass between the sidewalk and the road is the *parking,* and you might drive to the store to pick up some *pickles*—not cucumbers preserved in brine, but *pickle cards:* pull-tab lottery cards (cousins of the *scratch-offs* you might find elsewhere).

Gambling in America is a state-regulated industry, which is why this term, similar to some of the words for roads or drive-through liquor stores, tends to stop abruptly at the state line. And the terms of use in Nebraska are explicitly set forth in the Nebraska Pickle Card Lottery Act (a real law), which specifies, among other things, that:

> A pickle card shall mean any disposable card, board, or ticket which accords a person an opportunity to win a cash prize by opening, pulling, detaching, or otherwise removing one or more tabs from the card, board, or ticket to reveal a set of numbers, letters, symbols, or configurations, or any combination thereof.

According to the Nebraska Charitable Gaming Division, the term derives from when the cards were illegal, and bartenders would store them "in large empty 'pickle jars' which could easily be skirted out of sight."

HOW TO PRETEND YOU'RE FROM

MICHIGAN

Of everyone nationwide who says *Devil's Night, fireflies,* and *pop,* 85 percent of them come from Michigan. Another way to think of it: if you meet a random American who uses these three terms, there's an 85 percent chance that you're talking to someone from Michigan.

Michiganders often distinguish between the Lower and Upper Peninsulas of their state. Linguistically, however, the state is one. The denizens of the Upper Peninsula (*yoopers*), while having their own linguistic quirks, are still closer in dialect to mainland Michigan than anywhere else. The Mackinac Bridge, which connects the two peninsulas, is not much of a dividing line. Only once you cross through the Hiawatha National Forest and emerge on the other side do the people begin to speak more like their neighbors in Wisconsin.

HOW TO PRETEND YOU'RE FROM

PHILADELPHIA

Philadelphia is only a couple of hours away from New York, but the speech in the two cities is sharply different—which may well be a reflection of the cities' ages. They were both urban centers long before cars and trains brought them closer together. In addition to its distinct accent, in Philadelphia you'll find *pillbugs, jimmies* on ice cream, *hoagies* (not *subs*), and *Mischief Night,* the night before Halloween. You might hear the word *jawn* as a stand-in for just about anything (similar in some respects to the use of *da kine* in Hawaii), and, during the summer, you don't go *to the beach,* you go *down the shore*.

Philadelphia is also, along with New York and Boston, one of the places you're least likely to encounter someone who pronounces *Mary, merry,* and *marry* the same. If all three words are pronounced differently or if *Mary* and *merry* sound the same but *marry* is distinct, you're most likely from around this area.

Philadelphia speech fades sharply as you move west over the Alleghenies into the area affectionately (or not) referred to as Pennsyltucky, before the Pittsburgh dialect begins to take over. But the Philadelphia influence can definitely be heard as you head east into New Jersey, a state that doesn't really have a dialect of its own but is rather sharply divided between Philadelphia-influenced South Jersey and New York–influenced North Jersey. The line between the two stretches diagonally from northwest to southeast, running just north of Trenton, along the northern boundary of Burlington County, down toward Atlantic City.

If you find yourself in this region, be sure to stop for a *cheesesteak,* a sandwich on a long roll laden with chopped steak and topped with cheese—sometimes American or provolone, but often Cheez Whiz (or just *wiz*), a gooey orange cheese-like substance. What elsewhere might be called *Italian ice* here is simply *water ice,* which, when said with a Philadelphia accent, usually sounds closer to *wooderice*.

HOW TO PRETEND YOU'RE FROM

PITTSBURGH

Because the modern age has erased many of the local boundaries that once existed—with the spread of chain restaurants, cable television, and, of course, the web—many people yearn to recover a sense of belonging and of place. That's why they often turn to their local dialects as a source of pride. Perhaps nowhere else exemplifies this as much as Pittsburgh, a city that, like Boston and Philadelphia, is proud of its distinctive speech.

When I published an initial round of dialect maps online in 2013, they left out Pittsburgh's distinctive *yins*. It felt as if the entire city of Pittsburgh let me know about it.

The language in Pittsburgh still bears marks of the Scots-Irish immigrants who settled in the western foothills of the Alleghenies. Unlike in Philadelphia, on the other side of the Alleghenies, here *cot* and *caught* are pronounced the same. (To learn how this happens, see page 102.) As in Philadelphia, you'd get a *hoagie* here, but perhaps you'd tie it up with a *gumband* instead of a *rubber band*. A faucet is a *spicket*, a traffic light is a *redlight*, a chipmunk is a *ground squirrel*, and you might hear someone refer to *onion snow*—a late spring snowfall.

2

Part Two

WHAT WE EAT

WHAT WE CALL

A SANDWICH ON A LONG ROLL WITH MEATS AND CHEESES

The Hoagie:
Four Origin Stories, All Likely False

About 82 percent of the country calls a long sandwich with an assortment of meats and cheeses a *sub,* but in the area around Philadelphia and South Jersey, this sandwich is always a *hoagie.* While the true origins of the term have yet to be conclusively established, many theories have been suggested over the years. Here are four.

- The hoagie was originated by Al de Palma in the 1930s. Failing to find work as a musician following the Great Depression, de Palma opened a sandwich shop in 1936 and dubbed his sandwiches *hoggies*—a reference to the fact that you'd have to be a hog to eat one. Over time (due to the Philadelphia accent, de Palma insisted), *hoggies* came to sound like *hoagies*.
- During World War I, the American government contracted with American International Shipbuilding to build the largest shipyard in the world, located at the southern end of Philadelphia, on the shores of the Delaware River, in an area called Hog Island. The Italian immigrants—allegedly known as *hoggies*—who worked in the navy yard building ships for the war effort would bring sandwiches loaded with meat, cheese, lettuce, tomatoes, peppers, and oil on a long submarine roll: the hoggie sandwich. At some point, *sandwich* was dropped, the short *o* sound became a long *o,* and the *hoagie* was born. (It's worth noting that the shipbuilding facilities at Hog Island had shut down some fifteen years before the first appearance of the word *hoggie* in 1936.)
- Howard Robboy, a sociology professor at the College of New Jersey and an expert in the history of the hoagie (yes, people do study such things), offered another explanation

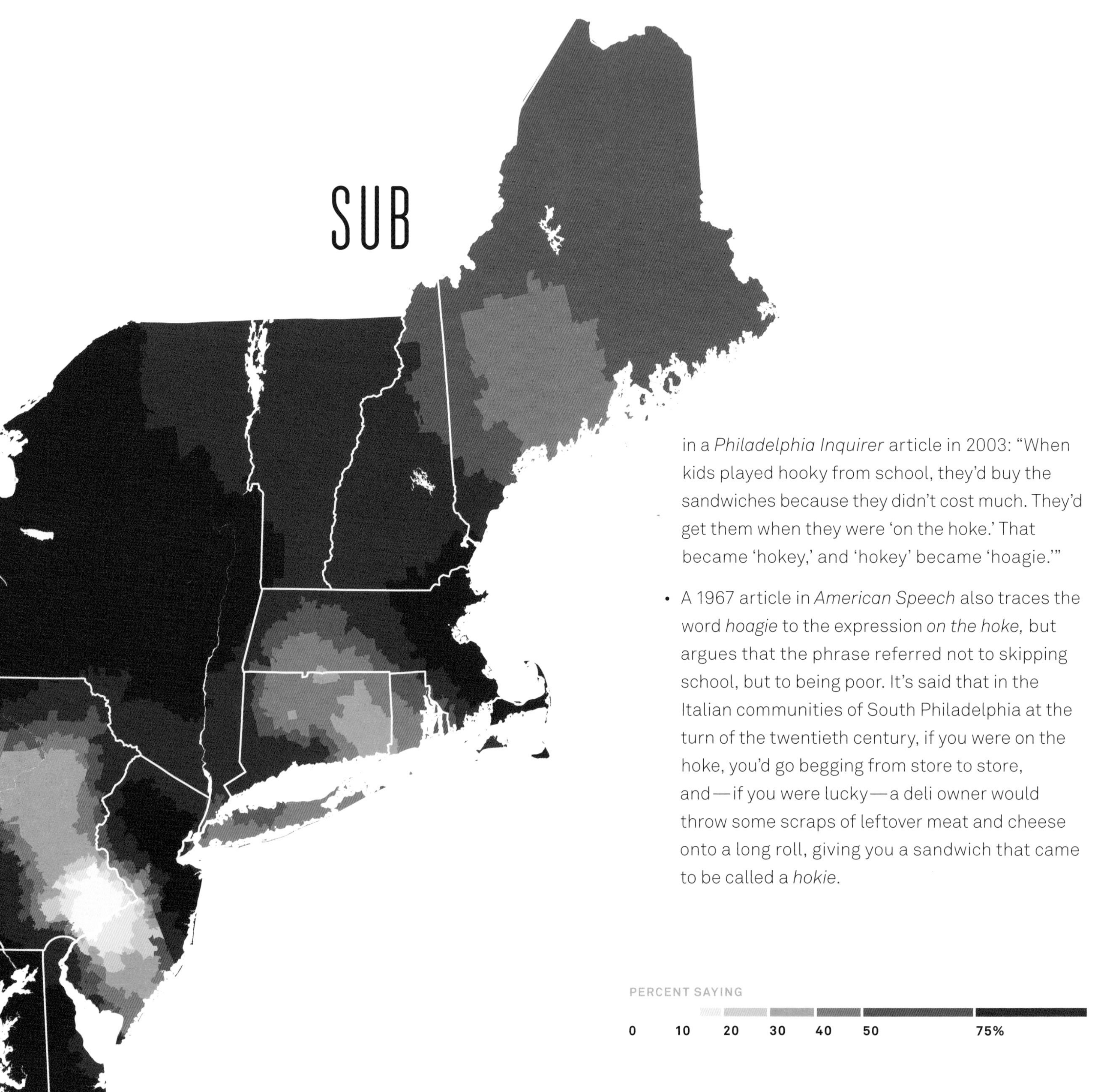

in a *Philadelphia Inquirer* article in 2003: "When kids played hooky from school, they'd buy the sandwiches because they didn't cost much. They'd get them when they were 'on the hoke.' That became 'hokey,' and 'hokey' became 'hoagie.'"

- A 1967 article in *American Speech* also traces the word *hoagie* to the expression *on the hoke,* but argues that the phrase referred not to skipping school, but to being poor. It's said that in the Italian communities of South Philadelphia at the turn of the twentieth century, if you were on the hoke, you'd go begging from store to store, and—if you were lucky—a deli owner would throw some scraps of leftover meat and cheese onto a long roll, giving you a sandwich that came to be called a *hokie*.

HOAGIE
HERO
WEDGE
GRINDER
ITALIAN SANDWICH

PANCAKES

Turns out, almost no one says *flapjacks* anymore.

WE ALL AGREE THEY'RE CALLED *PANCAKES,* BUT HOW DO WE DESCRIBE WHAT WE'RE POURING OVER THEM?

Americans are split fairly evenly on the question of whether syrup is pronounced *sir-up* or *seer-up,* with a less stark geographical divide than for many of the other language splits in this book. A slight majority goes to *sir-up* (53 percent). The long *e seer-up* is rarer (36 percent), concentrated in southern New England and the Mid-Atlantic states, most strongly in Pennsylvania, just north of Philadelphia.

SEER-UP

SIR-UP

SEER-UP

CARBONATION WITH AN IDENTITY CRISIS

Sometimes the boundaries between terms are fuzzier. In **OKLAHOMA**, *soda*, *pop*, and *coke* all mix together. Contrast this with the sharp boundary dividing **MILWAUKEE** *soda* territory from the *pop* country of northern **ILLINOIS**.

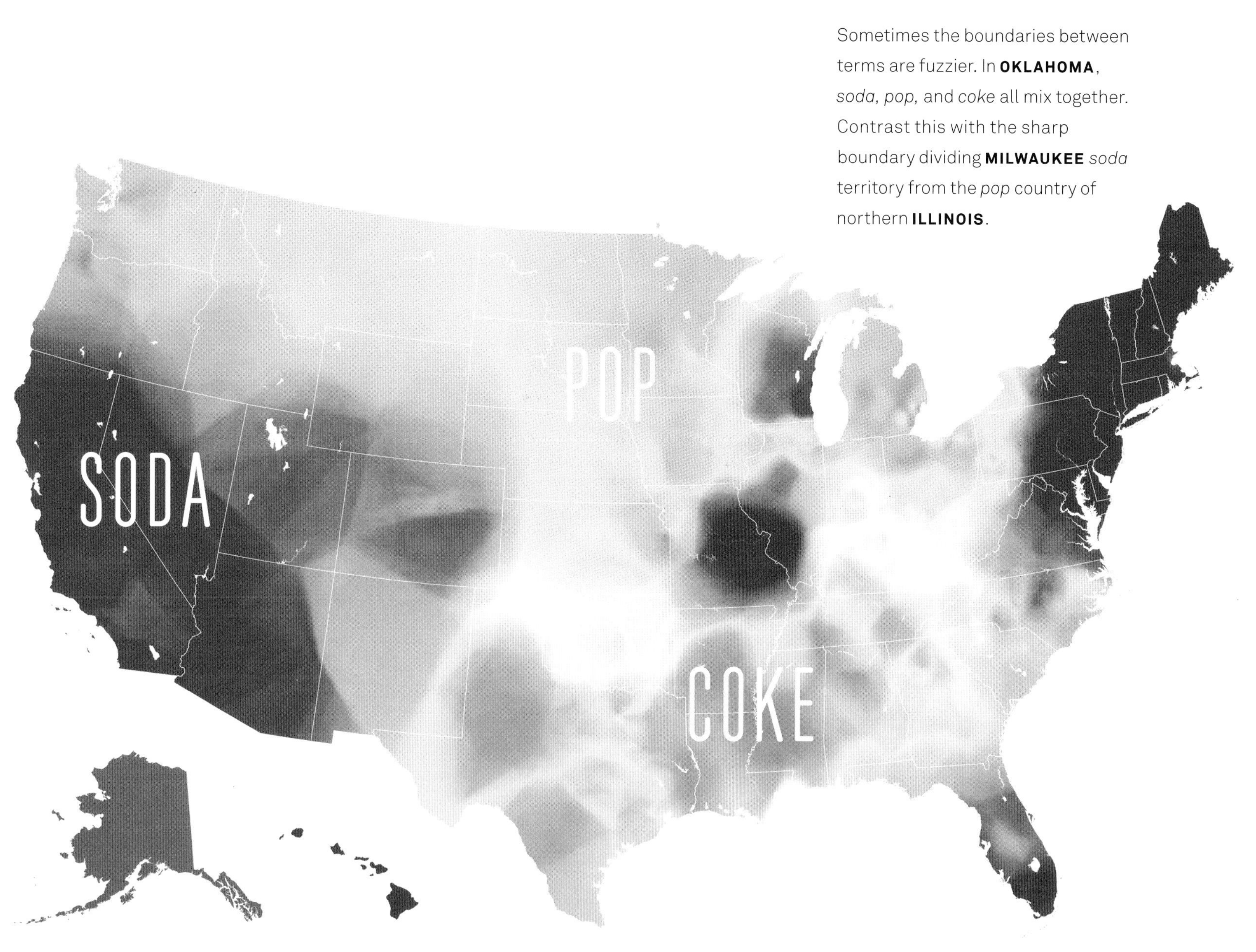

SODA 59%

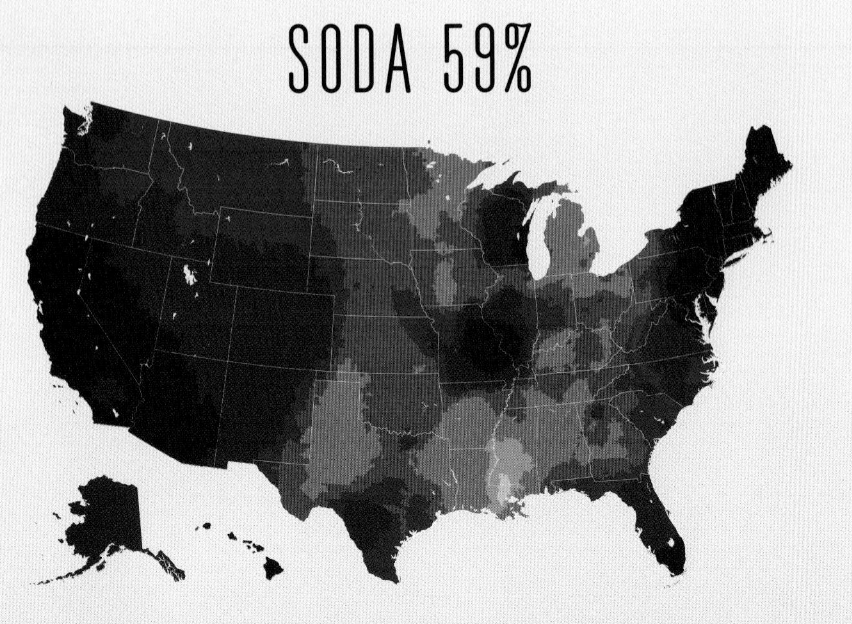

POP 18%

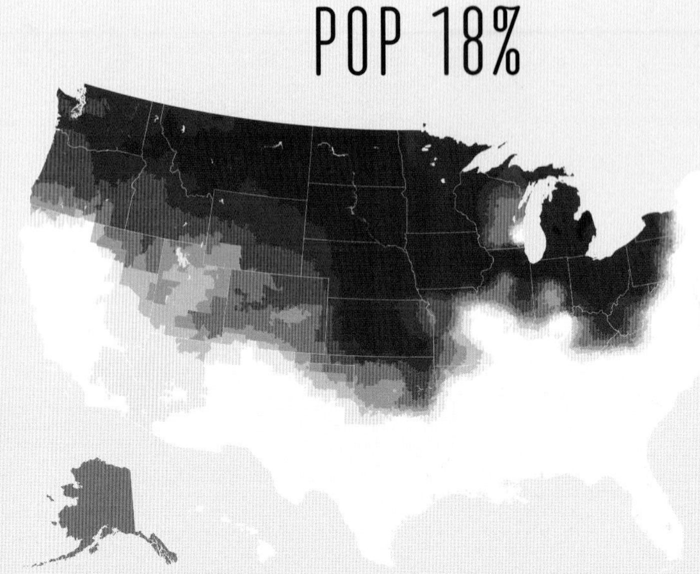

COKE 17%

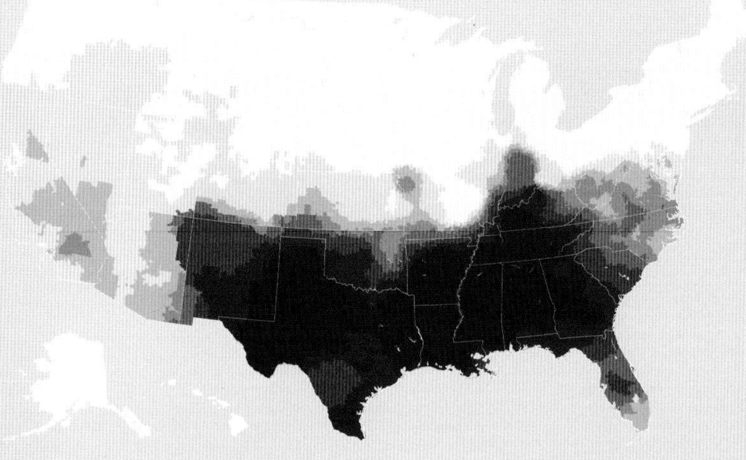

SOFT DRINK 6%

PERCENT SAYING

0 10 20 30 40 50 75%

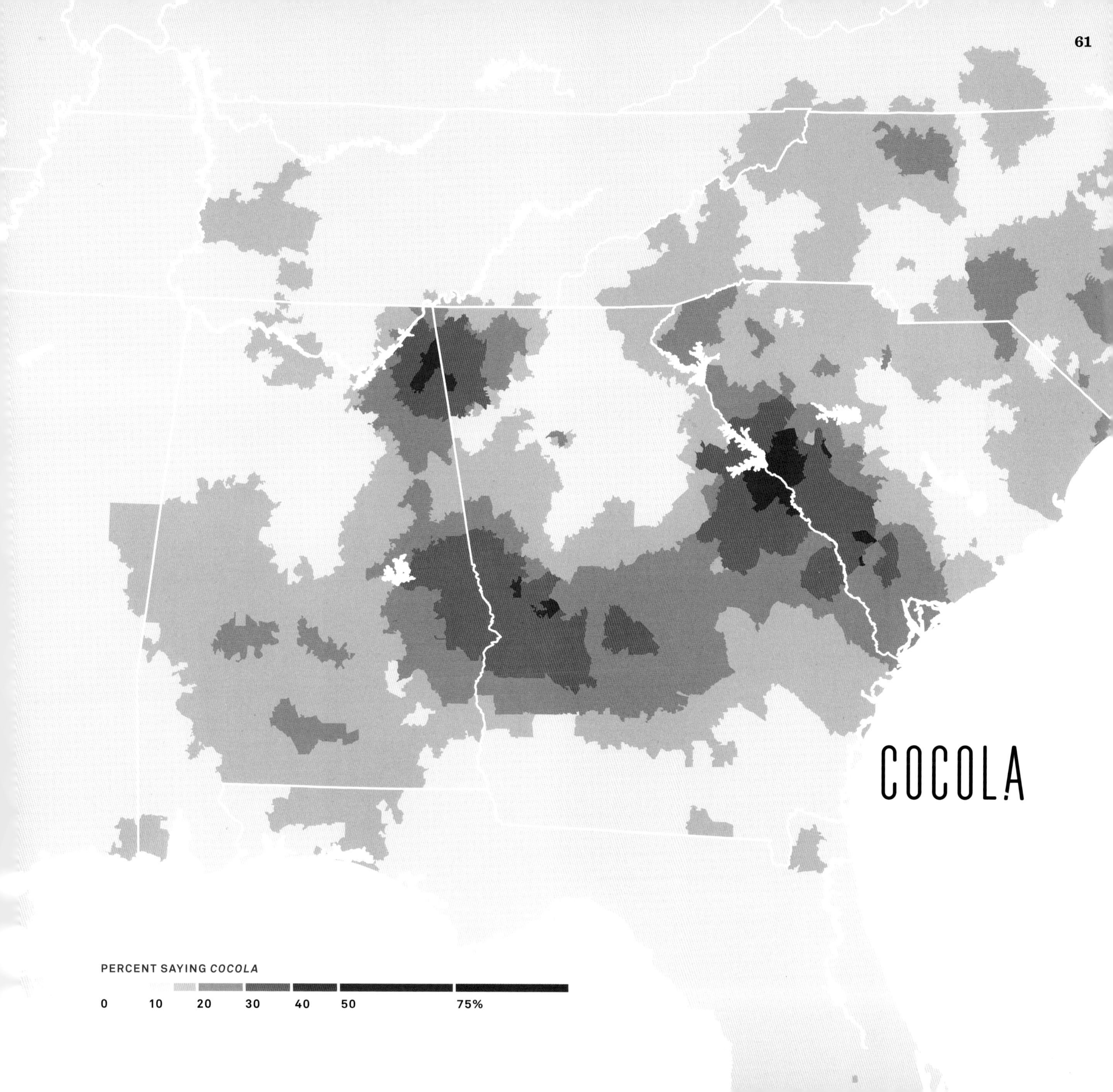

COCOLA

PERCENT SAYING *COCOLA*

0 10 20 30 40 50 75%

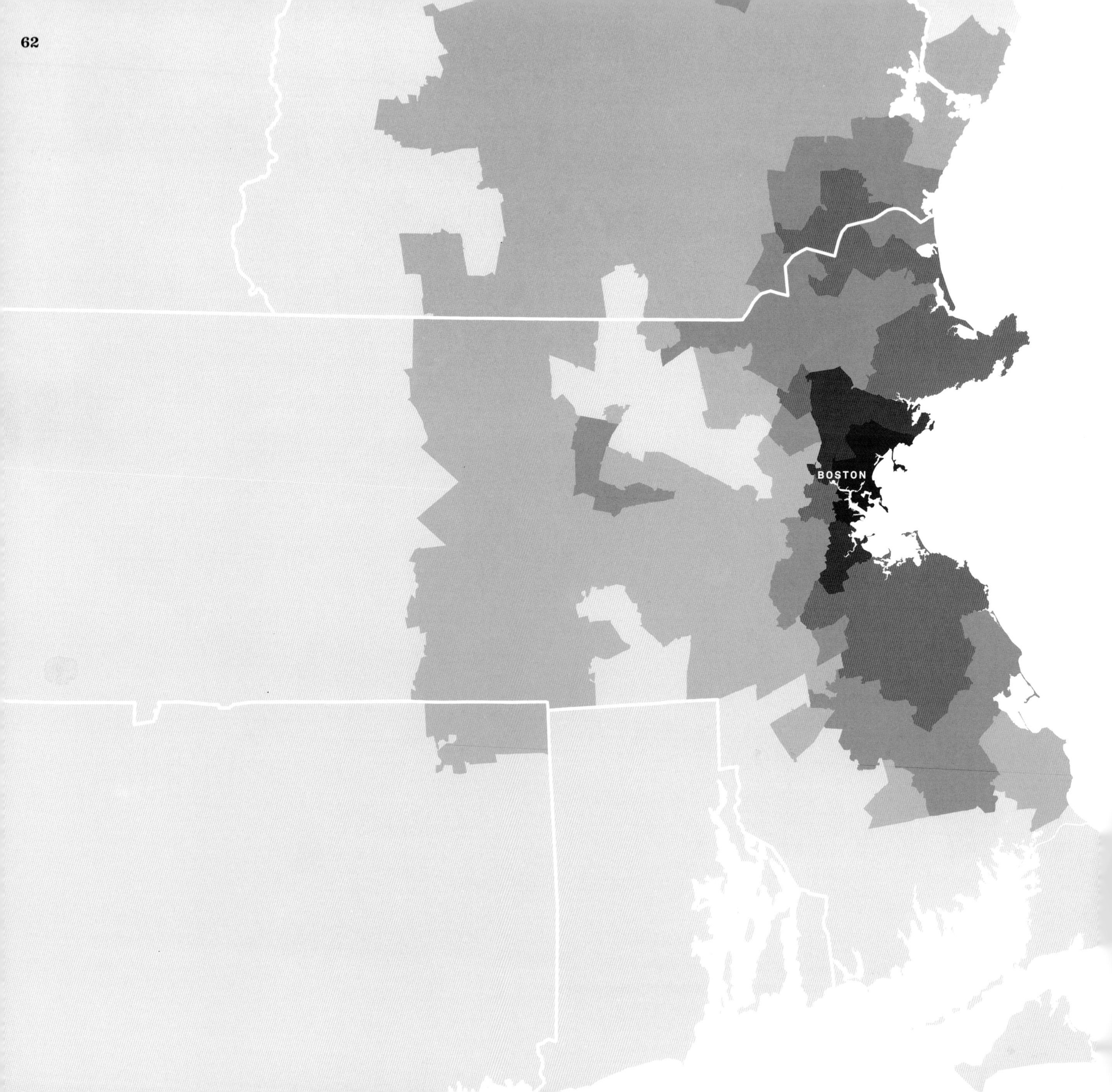
BOSTON

TONIC

Previously a common phrase in the Boston area, the use of *tonic* as the general word for a soft drink is on the decline.

While over 30 percent of Massachusetts residents born in the 1940s say *tonic*, almost none of the younger generation does: over 95 percent of those under the age of twenty-five say *soda*.

PERCENT SAYING *TONIC*

0 5 10 15 20 >25%

WHAT DO YOU CALL THIS?

The country can't quite get on the same page regarding how to pronounce the name of this vegetable. While the majority pronounces it *kaw-lih-flower,* a little over one in four people say *kaw-lee-flower,* most of whom are concentrated in the **NORTHEAST**.

WHAT DO YOU CALL THESE?

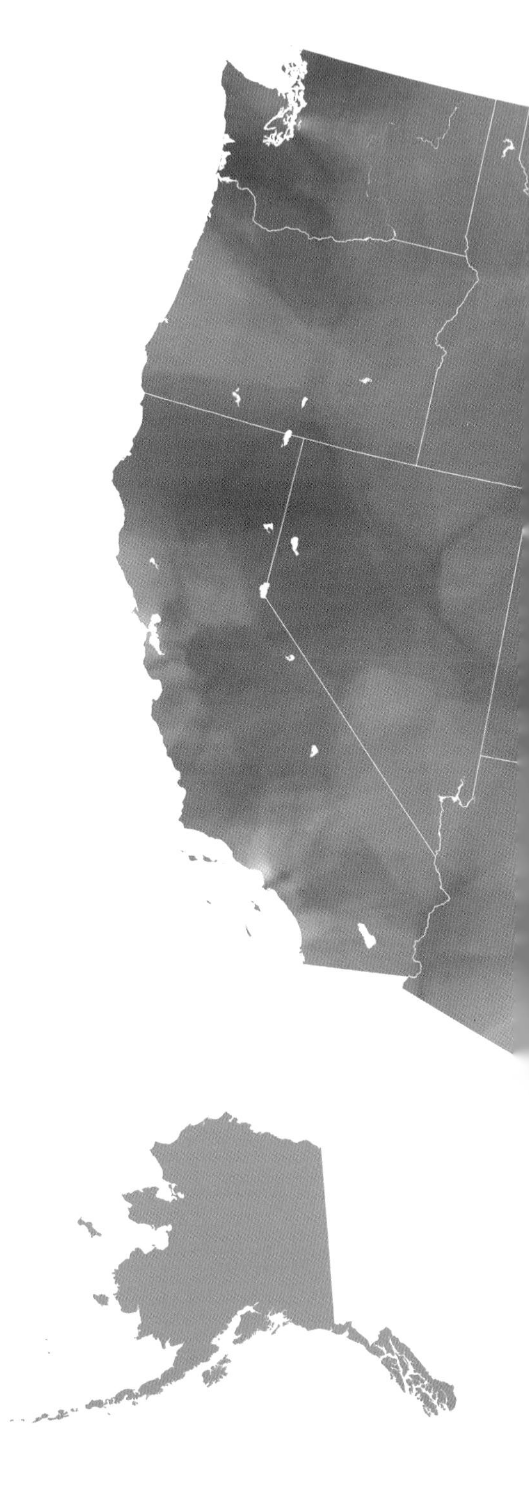

SCALLIONS
GREEN ONIONS
SCALLIONS

PLEASE BE MORE SPECIFIC ABOUT THIS PILE OF SHREDDED VEGETABLES

The *stoop sale* was far from the only contribution the Dutch settlers of New Amsterdam made to American English: *cookies* (from *koekjes,* meaning little cakes), *waffles* (*wafels*), *boss* (*baas,* meaning master), and perhaps even *Yankee* all derive from Dutch. So does the blend of shredded cabbage that the Dutch called *koolsla*—a combination of *kool* (cabbage) and *sla* (salad).

The anglicized *cold slaw* appears in written works as early as 1794, with the spelling *coleslaw* (or *cole-slaw*) developing in the mid-1800s. These days, in parts of the southern United States, the *cole* is often dropped, and the food is referred to just as *slaw*. The shortened form is most common in North Carolina, where more than 90 percent of people use it. It is least common in parts of California, where more than two-thirds of people stick with the full *coleslaw*.

The Great Cole Divide has as much an **EAST/WEST** division as a **NORTH/SOUTH** one. Resistance to the use of *slaw* as shorthand for *coleslaw* increases in the western part of the country, peaking in **HAWAII**, where 70 percent would not do so, including 16 percent who had never before heard of such a crazy idea.

As for the **NORTH/SOUTH** divide, it mirrors many of the language divisions seen so far, with one exception: here the *slaw*-only group has pushed well north of *y'all* territory into **MISSOURI**, **INDIANA**, and southern **ILLINOIS**.

WHAT DO YOU EAT WHEN YOU DON'T FEEL LIKE COOKING?

CARRY-OUT 24%

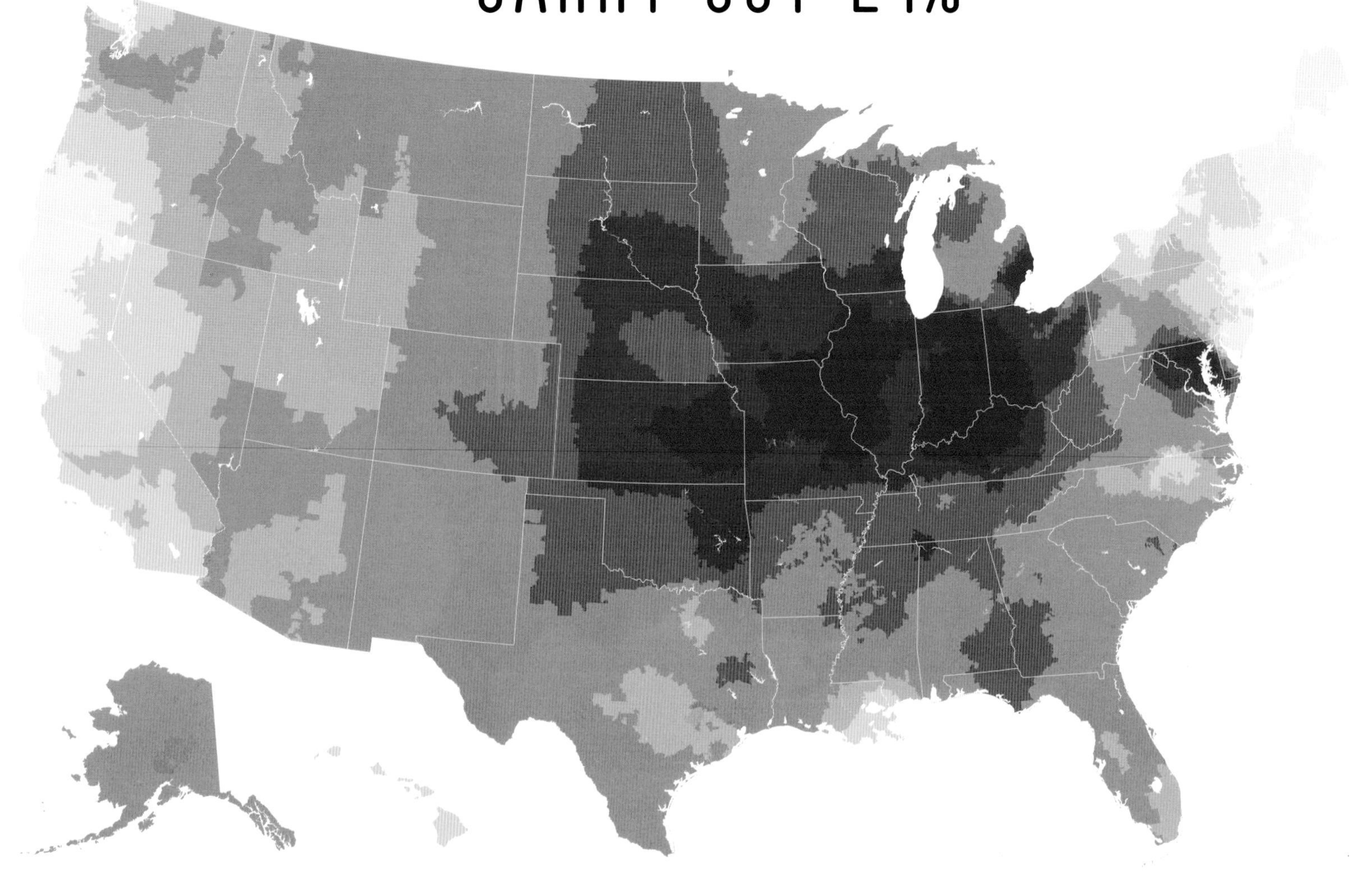

PERCENT SAYING

0 10 20 30 40 50 75%

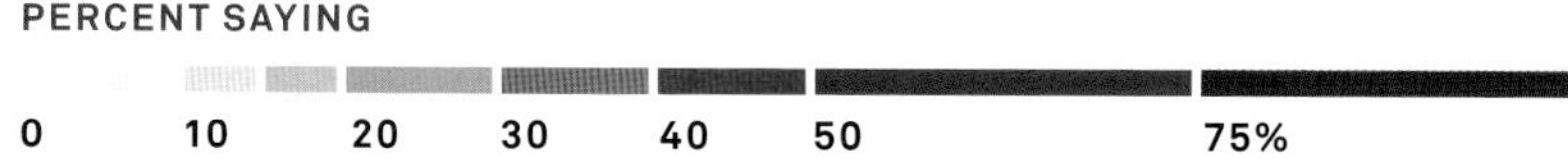

TAKEOUT 72%

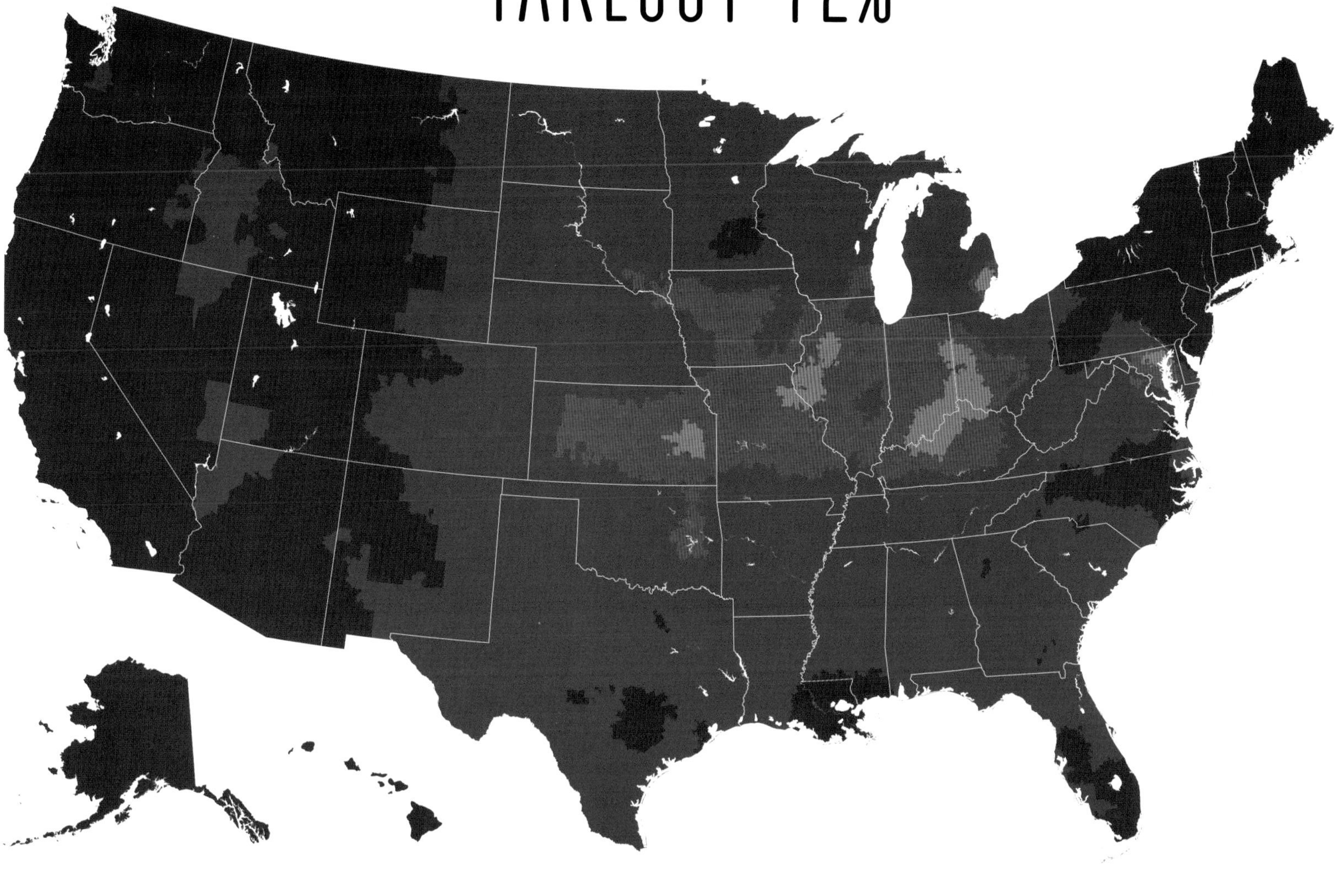

In most of the United States it's *takeout*, but in a swath of the **MIDDLE OF THE COUNTRY**—plus **WASHINGTON, D.C.**, and **DETROIT**—it's *carry-out*.

CARRY-OUT

WHAT DO YOU CALL THIS?

APE-RICOT

APP-RICOT

WHAT WE DRINK FROM AT SCHOOL

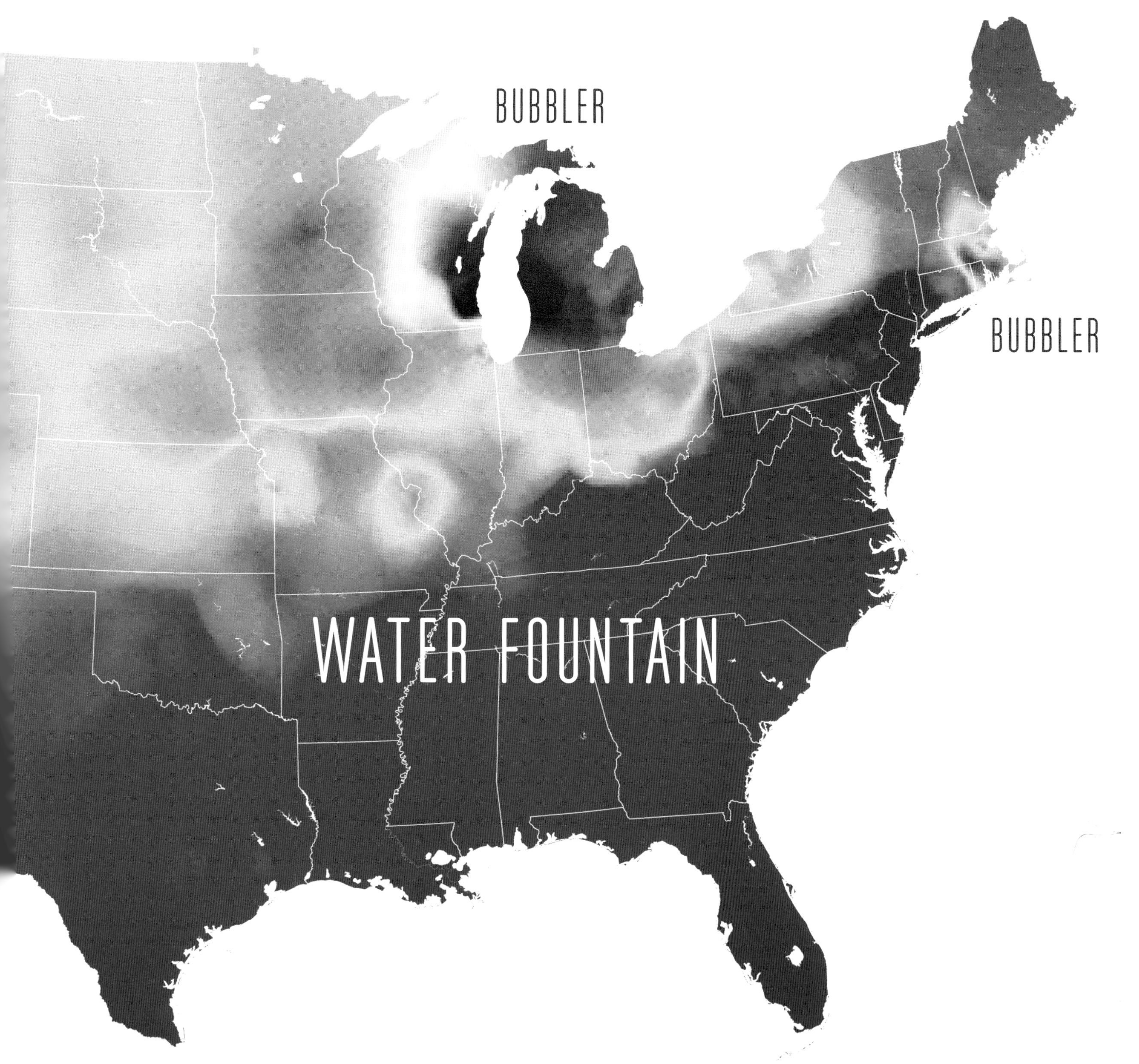
BUBBLER
BUBBLER
WATER FOUNTAIN

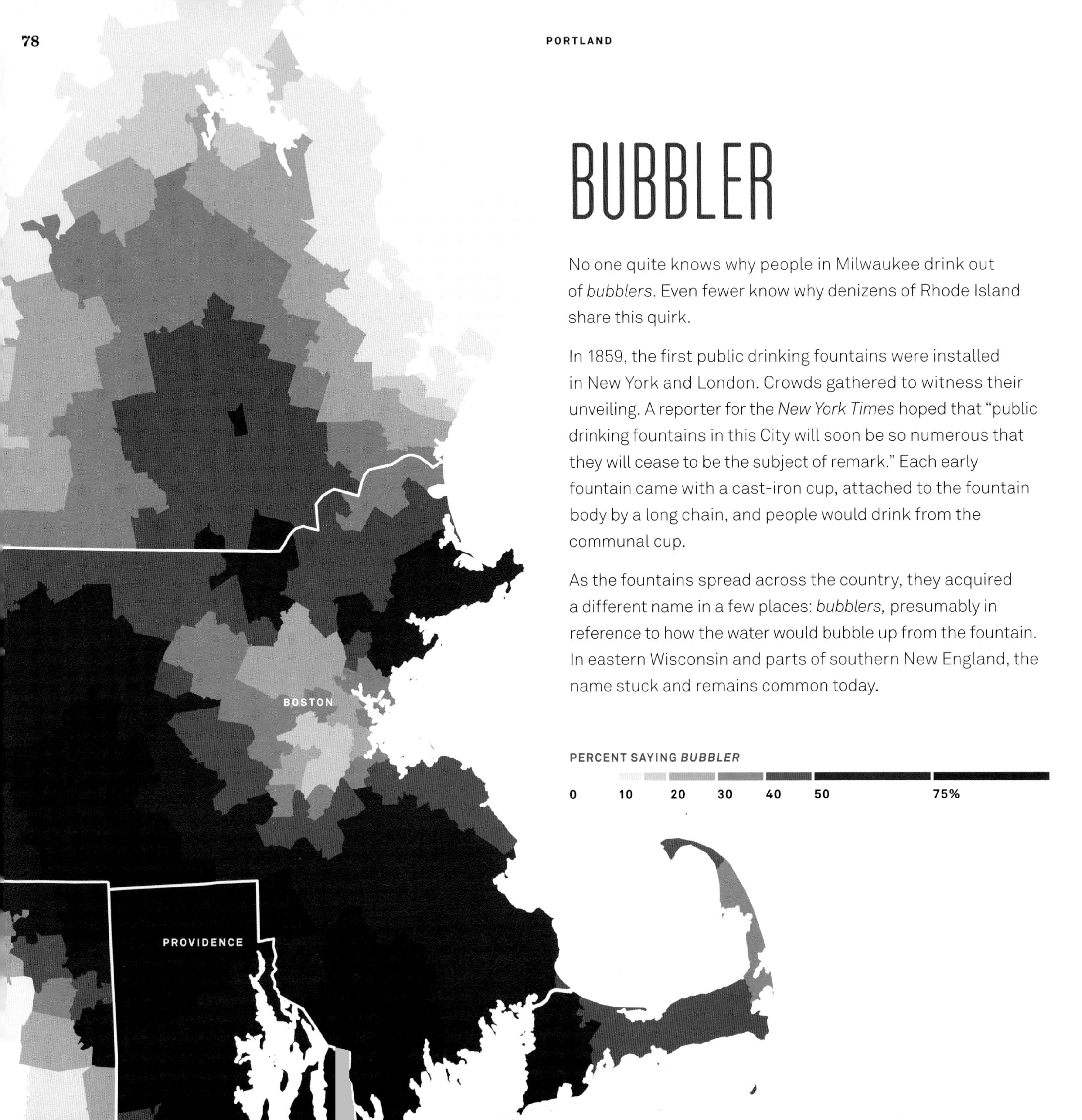

BUBBLER

No one quite knows why people in Milwaukee drink out of *bubblers*. Even fewer know why denizens of Rhode Island share this quirk.

In 1859, the first public drinking fountains were installed in New York and London. Crowds gathered to witness their unveiling. A reporter for the *New York Times* hoped that "public drinking fountains in this City will soon be so numerous that they will cease to be the subject of remark." Each early fountain came with a cast-iron cup, attached to the fountain body by a long chain, and people would drink from the communal cup.

As the fountains spread across the country, they acquired a different name in a few places: *bubblers,* presumably in reference to how the water would bubble up from the fountain. In eastern Wisconsin and parts of southern New England, the name stuck and remains common today.

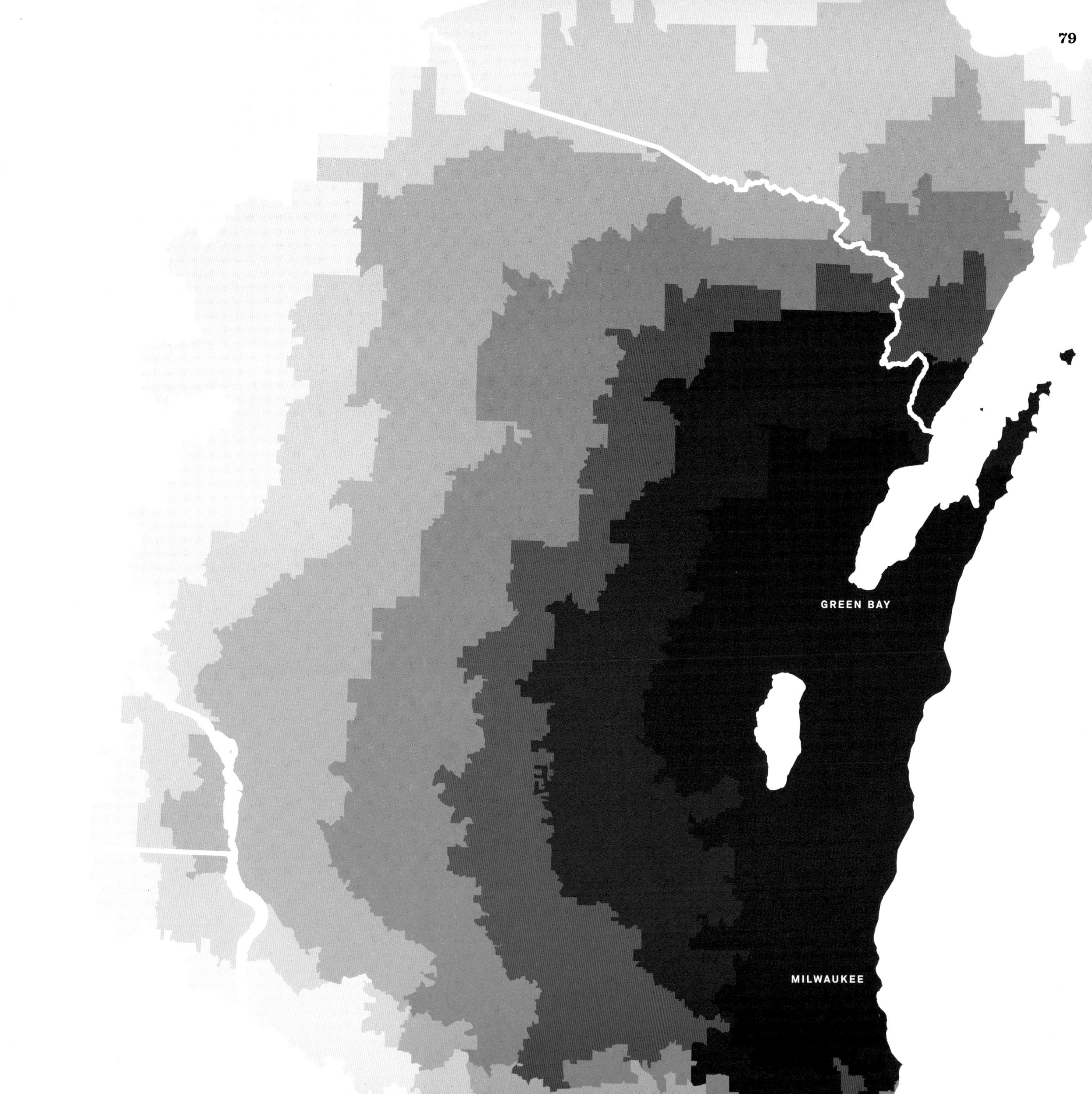
GREEN BAY
MILWAUKEE

HOW DO YOU SAY *PECAN*?

PIH-*KAHN* 39%

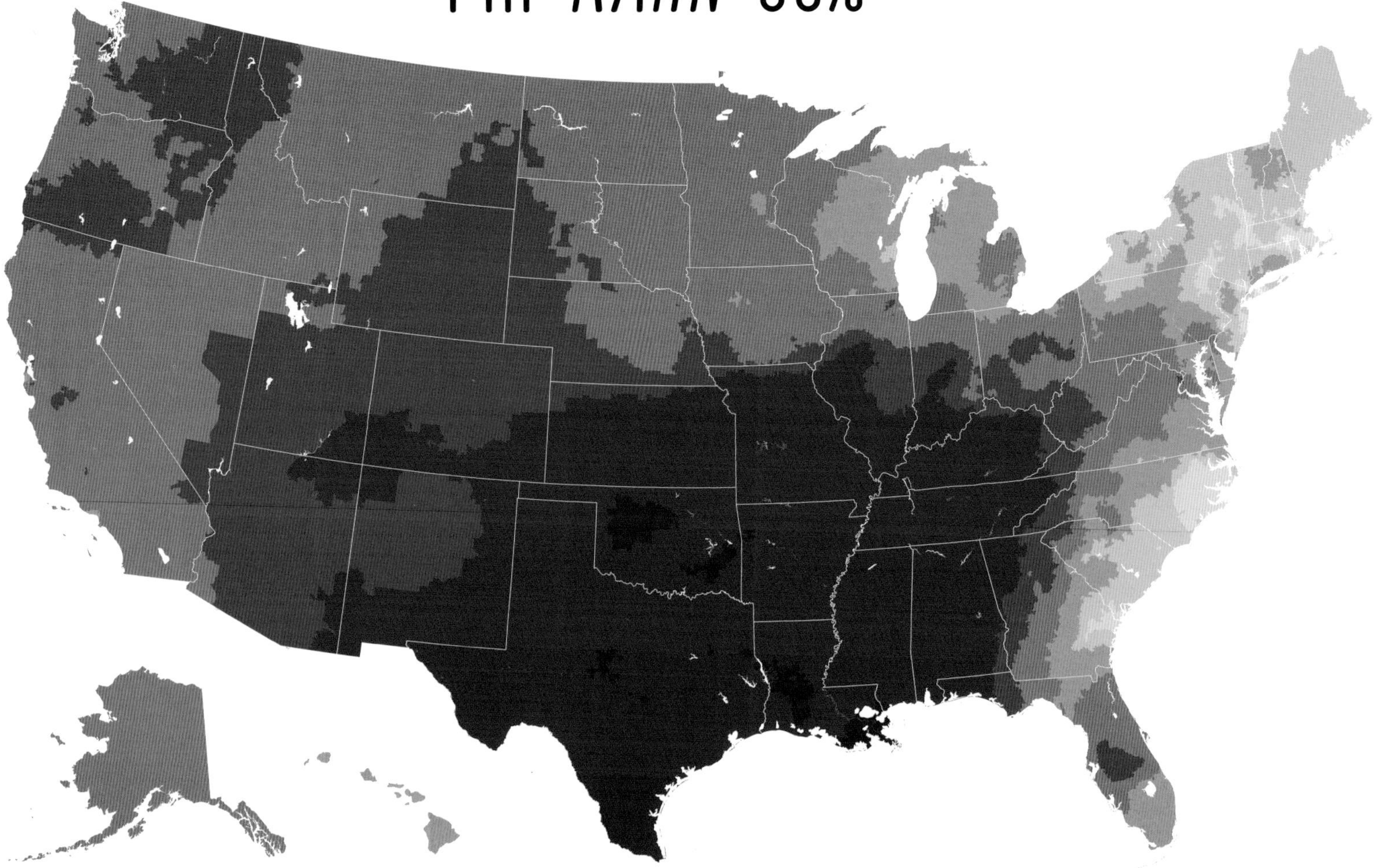

PEE-*KAHN* 16%

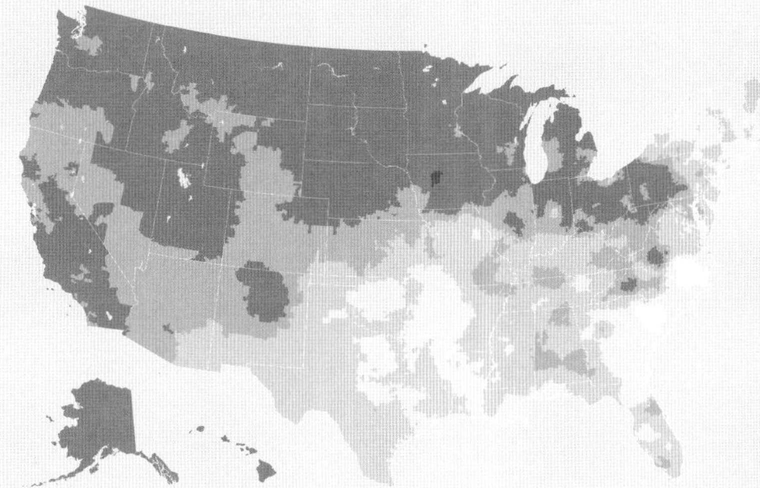

PEE-KAN 12%

PEE-KAHN 9%

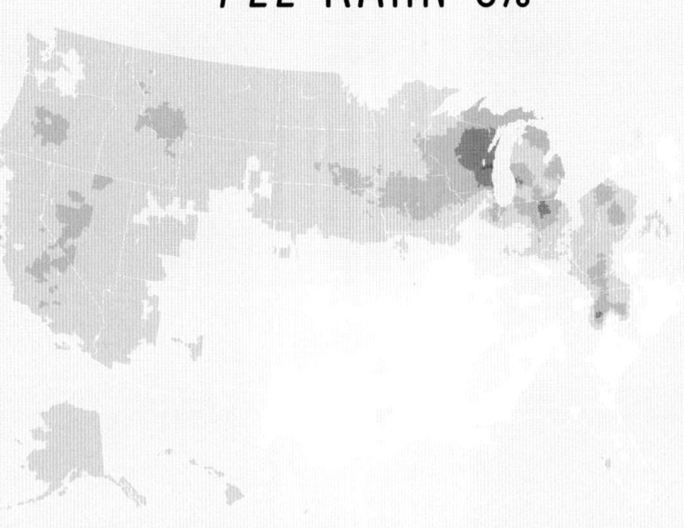

PEE-*KAN* 9%

HOW MANY SYLLABLES ARE THERE IN *CARAMEL*?

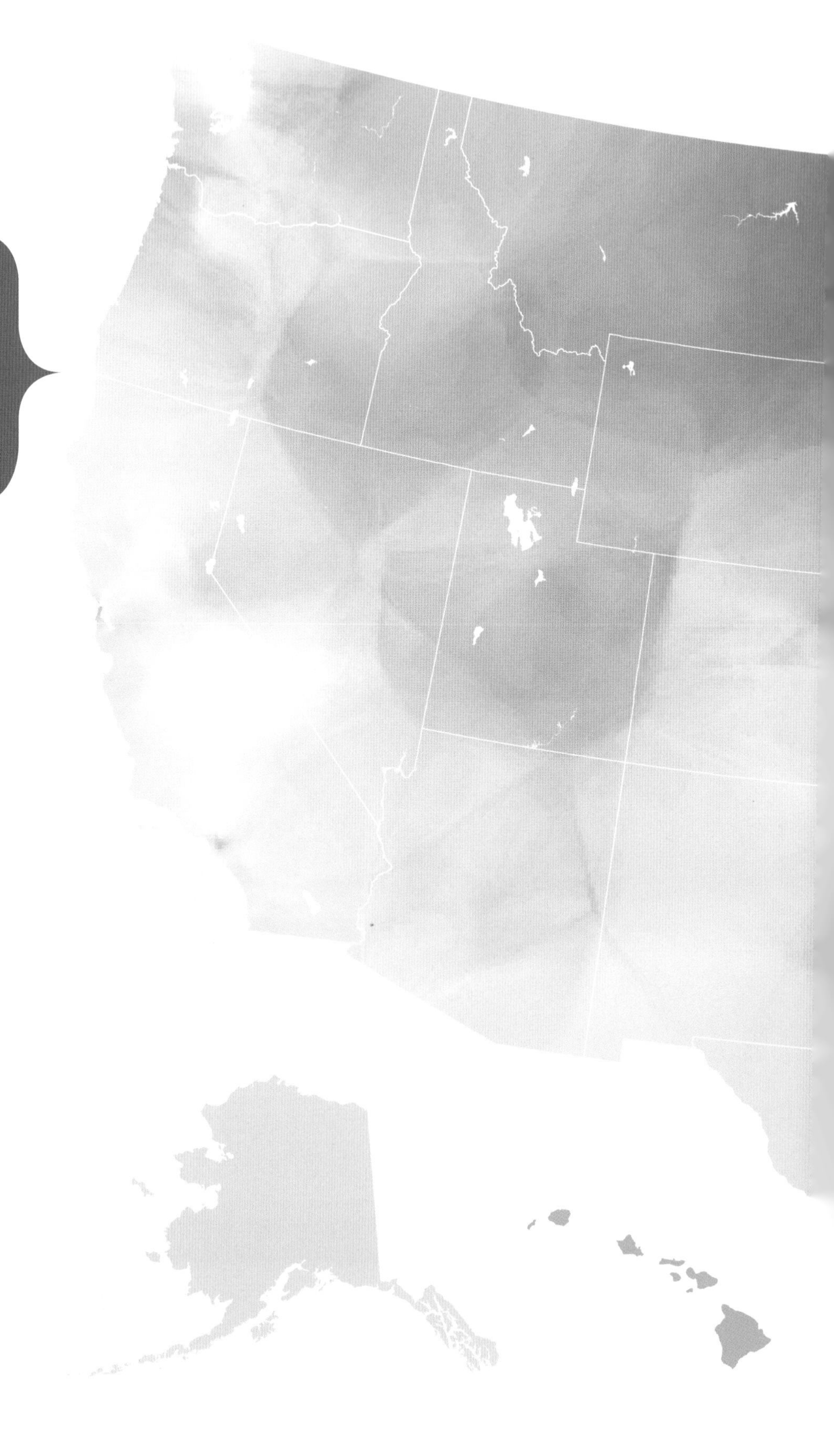

TWO
THREE

CAN YOU USE *FROSTING* AND *ICING* INTERCHANGEABLY?

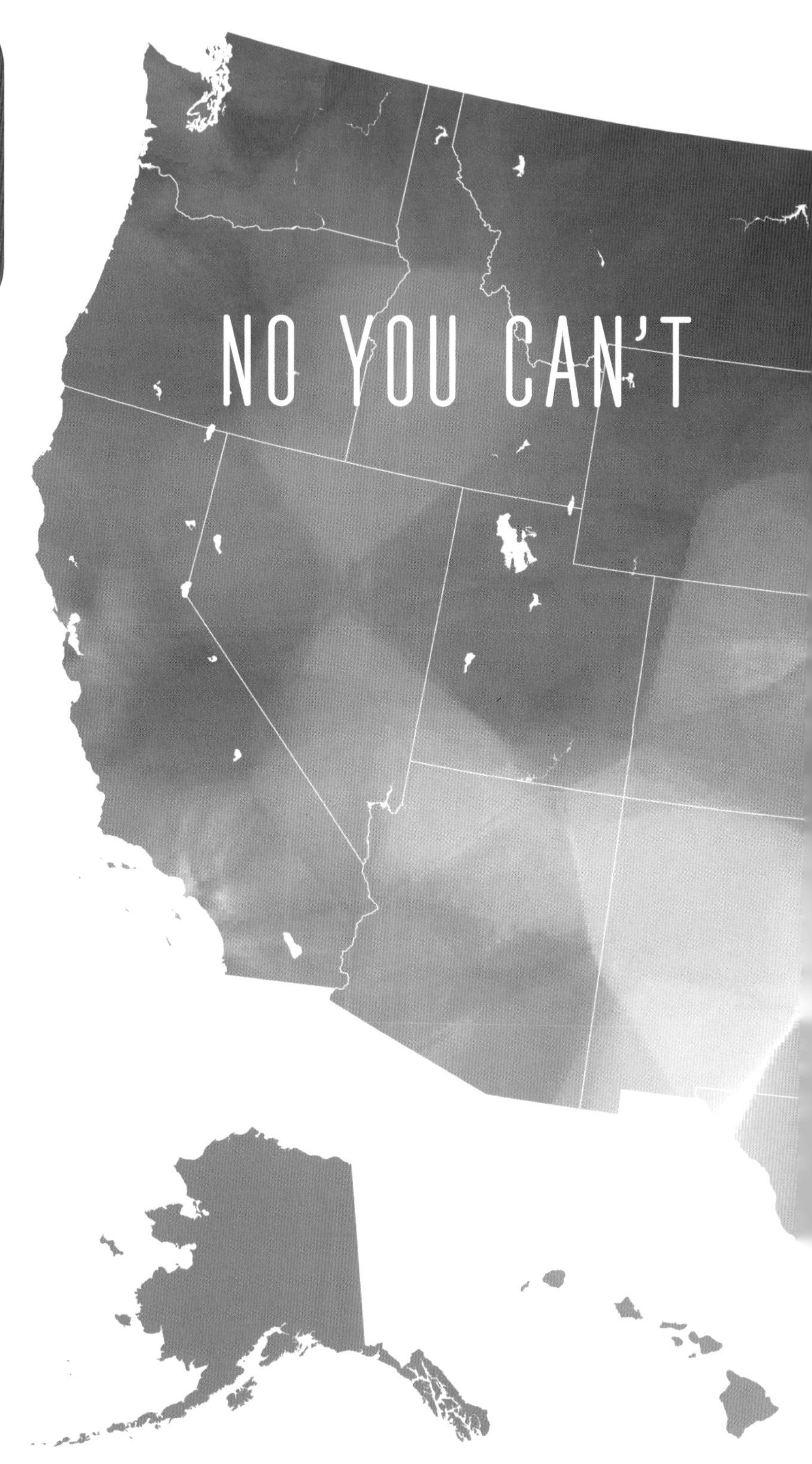

For what it's worth, the *Associated Press Stylebook*—a veritable bible in many newsrooms—somewhat pedantically insists that *frosting* is the term to use for cupcake and cake topping, while *icing* should be reserved for the sugar decorations applied to cookies.

YES YOU CAN

THE GREAT DEBATE: *SPRINKLES* VS. *JIMMIES*

For almost the entire country, the hard bits of sugar on sundaes or cupcakes are *sprinkles,* but in South Jersey, eastern New England and, to a lesser extent, Pittsburgh and Milwaukee, they are often called *jimmies*. Especially around Boston, many argue that *jimmies* refers specifically to the chocolate version, while the other varities are indeed *sprinkles.*

According to the candy company Just Born (maker of Peeps), *jimmies* can be traced back to its original Brooklyn, New York, store, which opened in 1923, and the employee who first made them. He was Jimmy Bartholomew, and chocolate was long the only variety of sprinkle that he made and that Just Born sold. There is no credible evidence to corroborate this story, alas.

PERCENT SAYING

0 10 20 30 40 50 75%

Another legend holds that *jimmies* comes from the Jimmy Fund, a well-known Boston charity for cancer research that the Boston Red Sox have long supported. The charity was itself named after a young cancer patient... named Einar Gustafson, who was first introduced on the radio as Jimmy in order to protect his privacy. The claim is that a local ice cream store charged extra for ice cream with sprinkles on it and would then donate the money from the sale of the *jimmies* to the Jimmy Fund.

A persistent myth suggests that the word *jimmies* carries racist connotations, but, while the true origins of the word remain unclear, all research on the topic to date has failed to turn up any evidence of a racist past.

A more prosaic, and more plausible, story comes from language columnist Ben Zimmer, who notes that the word's origins can probably be traced to *jim-jams,* a term for small articles or knickknacks that has been around since the mid-sixteenth century.

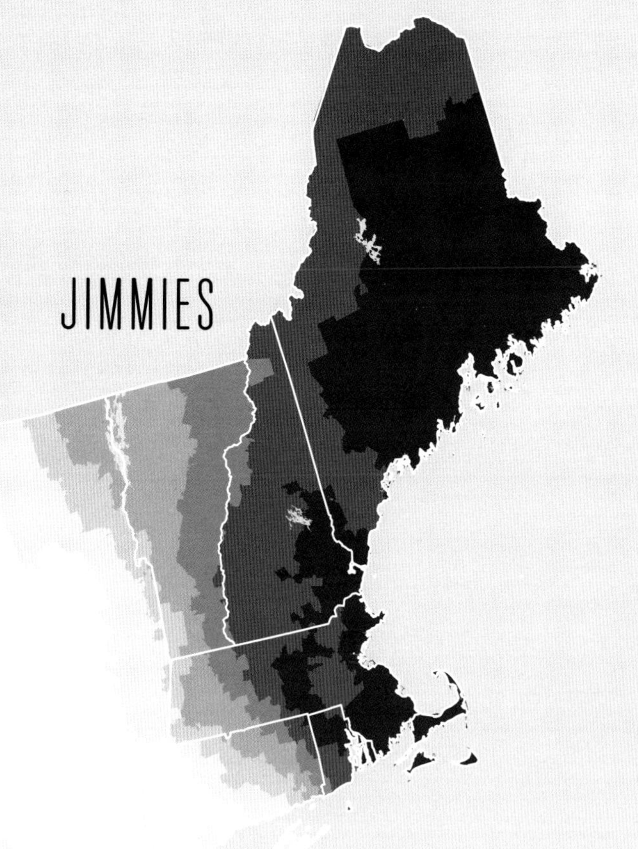

HOW TO PRETEND YOU'RE FROM

HAWAII

Nowhere in the United States is as linguistically diverse as Hawaii. Waves of Chinese-, Portuguese-, Japanese-, and English-speaking immigrants have all left their mark on the linguistics of the archipelago. It's the only state where the second most common language after English is not a European language. It is instead Tagalog, a language native to the Philippines. The U.S. Census Bureau estimates that fully a quarter of the Hawaiian population speaks a language other than English at home.

For a few thousand people, that language is Hawaiian, a Polynesian language spoken on the islands long before the arrival of English settlers in 1778. The use of Hawaiian decreased following English colonization of the islands, to the point at which it was almost lost entirely. But in the past several decades Hawaiian speakers have made a concerted effort to preserve and promote the language. Some schools offer immersion courses, many children learn Hawaiian as a second language, and it is now one of the official state languages of Hawaii (the other is English). But with so few native speakers of it, UNESCO still considers the language "critically endangered"—the highest degree of language endangerment, just short of extinction.

You're more likely to hear the locals speaking another language: Hawaii Pidgin English, which about half the population speaks to varying degrees. The language evolved out of a blend of Chinese, Japanese, English, and Hawaiian, and it continues to develop today. A translation of the Bible, by linguistics professor Joseph Grimes, gives a sense of how the language sounds. The translation, called *Da Jesus Book*, begins:

> Da time wen eryting had start, God wen make da sky an da world. Da world come so no mo notting inside, no mo shape notting. On top da wild ocean dat cova eryting, neva had light notting. Ony had God Spirit dea, moving aroun ova da watta.

The line between Pidgin and English is not always clear, as the English spoken in Hawaii is itself quite different from the English you'd hear on the *mainland*.

If you've done your work you're *pau hana* (or just *pau* for short), good food is *grinds*, and *da kine* is used for, well, just about anything. In Hawaii, flip-flops are *slippers*, goose bumps are *chicken skin*, and someone of European ancestry (or someone from the *mainland*) is a *haole*. Perhaps surprisingly, many subtleties of Hawaiian English are closer to the English spoken in England than that spoken in America. In Hawaii, for example, people are more likely to refer to a trash can as a *rubbish bin* than anywhere else in the United States.

HOW TO PRETEND YOU'RE FROM

ALASKA

When those from the *outside*—that is, the *Lower 48* states—first make their way to Alaska, they're known as *cheechakos*. Once they've been there a while, they're called *sourdoughs*.

Hooch, a word for illegally made or low-quality liquor, was introduced to the contiguous United States by miners returning from the Klondike gold rush in the late 1890s. It's a shortening of the Tlingit *hoochinoo,* an alcoholic drink made from rum and molasses. And if you're going to go out into *the bush,* watch out for the *williwaw* and *taku* winds and grab some food from the *cache* (a small food-storage cabin elevated high off the ground to keep bears out). And while we're on the subject, you'd do well to bring some *bear insurance* along with you—that is, a gun or two.

Alaska is home to the highest percentage of people—roughly one in twenty—who speak a Native North American language other than Navajo in the home. These languages include Yupik, Aleut, and Inupiat.

The debate over whether Native Alaskan languages really do have dozens of words for snow (which, of course, English has as well: *snow, sleet, flurries, slush, hail*) is a tricky one. Linguists seemed to debunk the hypothesis in the mid-'80s, but since then it has made something of a comeback. Some examples:

- *Piegnartoq* (good snow for driving your sled)
- *Qissuqaqtuq* (snow that has frozen overnight, becoming good for travel)
- *Apputtattuq* (snow that accumulates on newly formed ice and causes its thinning)
- *Aqilokoq* (softly falling snow)

HOW TO PRETEND YOU'RE FROM

THE PACIFIC NORTHWEST

A general feature of American dialects is that as you move south and west, farther from the original linguistic centers of colonial America, differences in speech patterns become more subtle. It's as true of the Pacific Northwest as it is of California.

The Pacific Northwest is notable for some of its odd juxtapositions: it's one of the smattering of places where *potato bug* is a common word for the woodlouse. In California you're more likely to hear *roly-poly, pillbug,* or *sow bug*. If you meet a random American who knows about *potato bugs,* knows that spinning a car in circles is *doing cookies,* and calls a mountain lion a *cougar,* there's more than an 80 percent chance that they're from Washington or Oregon.

Distinguishing among Washington, Oregon, and Northern California is a task all its own. One easy tip: in Washington you go *to the ocean,* while in Oregon you go *to the coast*. Meanwhile, in California you go *to the beach,* and way off in South Jersey you go *down the shore*. And Oregon is *doing cookies* territory, while Washington is definitely not.

HOW TO PRETEND YOU'RE FROM

COLORADO

Welcome to Colo-*rad*-oh (it's often pronounced *rad,* like *bad,* not *rahd,* like *rod*). Note too that the town north of Denver is pronounced *lewis-ville,* not *louie-ville,* as it is in Kentucky. Many towns have Spanish names, but few retain their Spanish pronunciations. Thus, Buena Vista is *byoo-nuh vista* (*byoo-nee* for short), Salida is *suh-lye-duh,* and Arriba is *air-uh-buh*.

If you're wondering why there are so many *parks* in Colorado town names, it derives from the French-Canadian fur trappers who settled the area in the nineteenth century. They called mountain valleys *parks* or, as in neighboring states like Wyoming, *holes* (as in Jackson Hole).

HOW TO PRETEND YOU'RE FROM

CALIFORNIA

Once you get *out west,* there aren't as many regional vocabulary quirks as *back east*. No one thing identifies someone as definitively Californian, but there are some clues: In California you find *freeways* and *big rigs*. You stop for some water at the *drinking fountain*.

Like many of the things in this book, the story of California's language is a story about two things: migration and media.

By nature, when two people with different accents converse, they unconsciously shift their speech patterns toward each other—almost averaging out their own speech patterns, in a way. So, for much of the early twentieth century, California speech sounded like a mish-mash of dialects from everywhere else. California was a giant blender of the rest of the country's speech: the general American dialect.

In the mid-twentieth century, though, national radio began to replace local radio for the first time. The voices in Americans' living rooms were, by and large, the voices of those in America's media and entertainment hub: Californians.

National media in the twentieth century and the Internet in the twenty-first do not remove geographical quirks or obliterate local speech patterns, but they do allow for linguistic innovation to spread far more rapidly and far more extensively than ever before.

In addition, migration into Southern California and the region's position at the heart of American media and entertainment production mean that many speech patterns that start in California are quick to catch on in the rest of the country. Surfer speak, valley girl, etc., all began as niche dialects in Los Angeles. Forty years ago, words like *dude, cool,* and *gnarly* weren't widely known. But when surfer culture developed in the 1970s and valley girl speech began to take shape in the 1980s, those ways of speaking quickly caught on elsewhere, thanks to national media.

3

Part Three

HOW WE SOUND

PUH-JAM-UHZ

WHAT WE WEAR TO SLEEP

HOW WE SAY *AUNT*

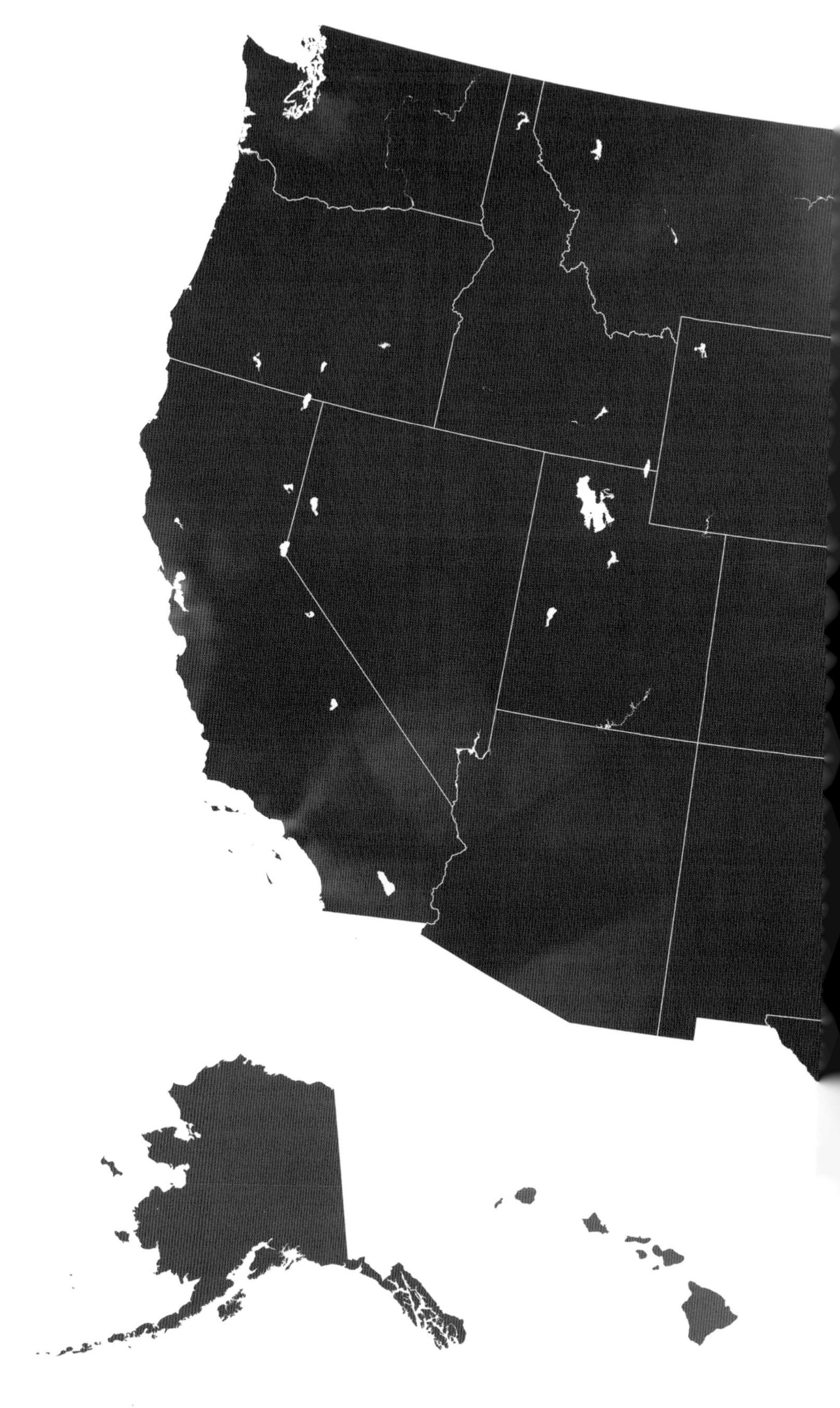

TO SOUND LIKE *AHNT*
TO SOUND LIKE *ANT*

DO YOU PRONOUNCE THE *T* IN *OFTEN*?

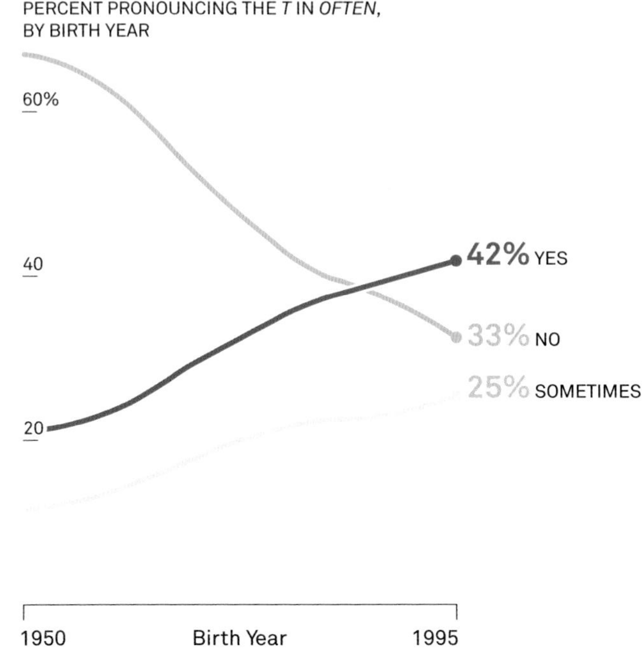

Despite the appearance of both pronunciations in most dictionaries, strict prescriptivists and pedants maintain that the only acceptable pronunciation for *often* is with a silent *t*.

The audible *t* pronunciation is not a recent invention, but rather a return to the original pronunciation of the word, harking back to when *often* first entered the English language as a modification of *oft*.

According to the *American Heritage Dictionary,* the audible *t* sound began to recede in the sixteenth and seventeenth centuries, as part of a broader trend of dropping consonants to make language easier to articulate.

The silent *t* version was the accepted pronunciation until the nineteenth century, when more people began to learn how to read. In an example of what linguists call a *spelling pronunciation,* people gradually began to pronounce the word as it's spelled, with the *t* and all. It's unclear why spelling pronunciations develop for some words and not others: note, words like *soften* and *listen* both retain their silent *t.*

These days, the pronunciation of *often* doesn't have a particularly striking geographic pattern. The use of the audible *t* is most common in Florida, where roughly half the population pronounces it, and least common in Minneapolis, Boston, and New York, where less than 20 percent does.

But there is a noticeable effect of age. Two-thirds of those born in the 1950s pronounce *often* with a silent *t,* compared to only one-third of those born in the 1990s. If the trend continues, it would appear that the silent *t* pronunciation is on its way out.

NO 48%

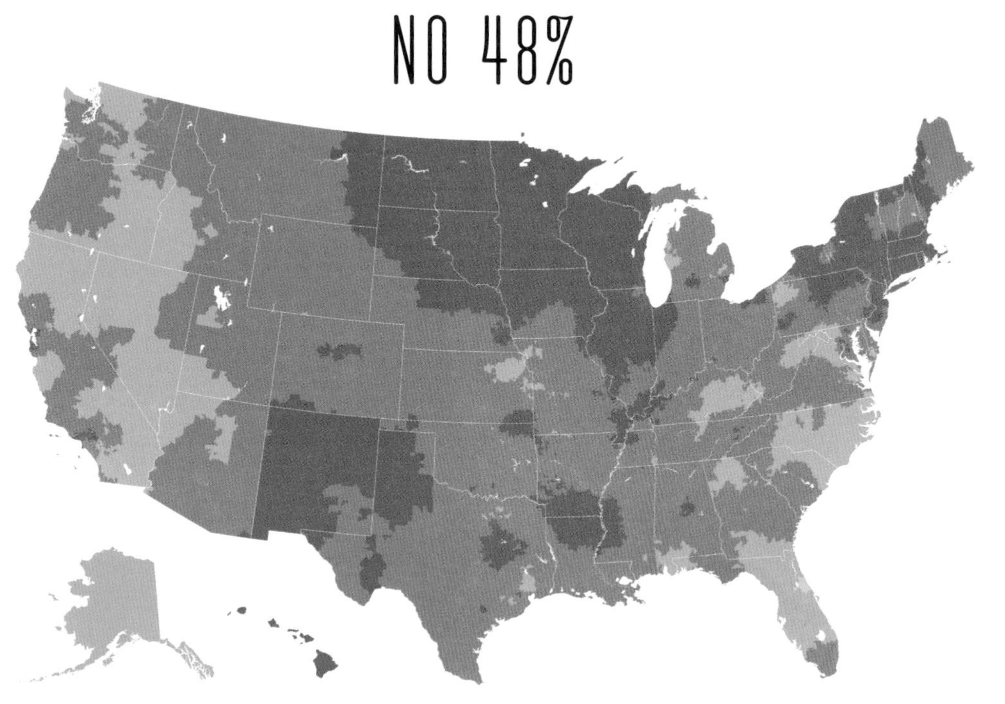

YES 33%

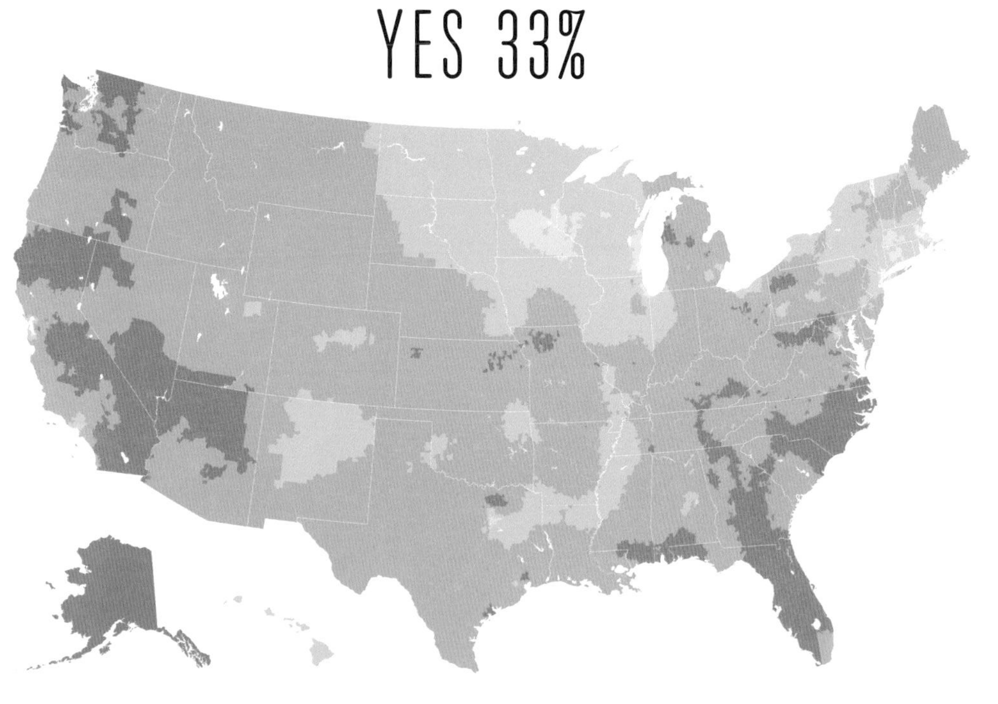

PERCENT SAYING

0 10 20 30 40 50 75%

WHEN TWO VOWELS BECOME ONE

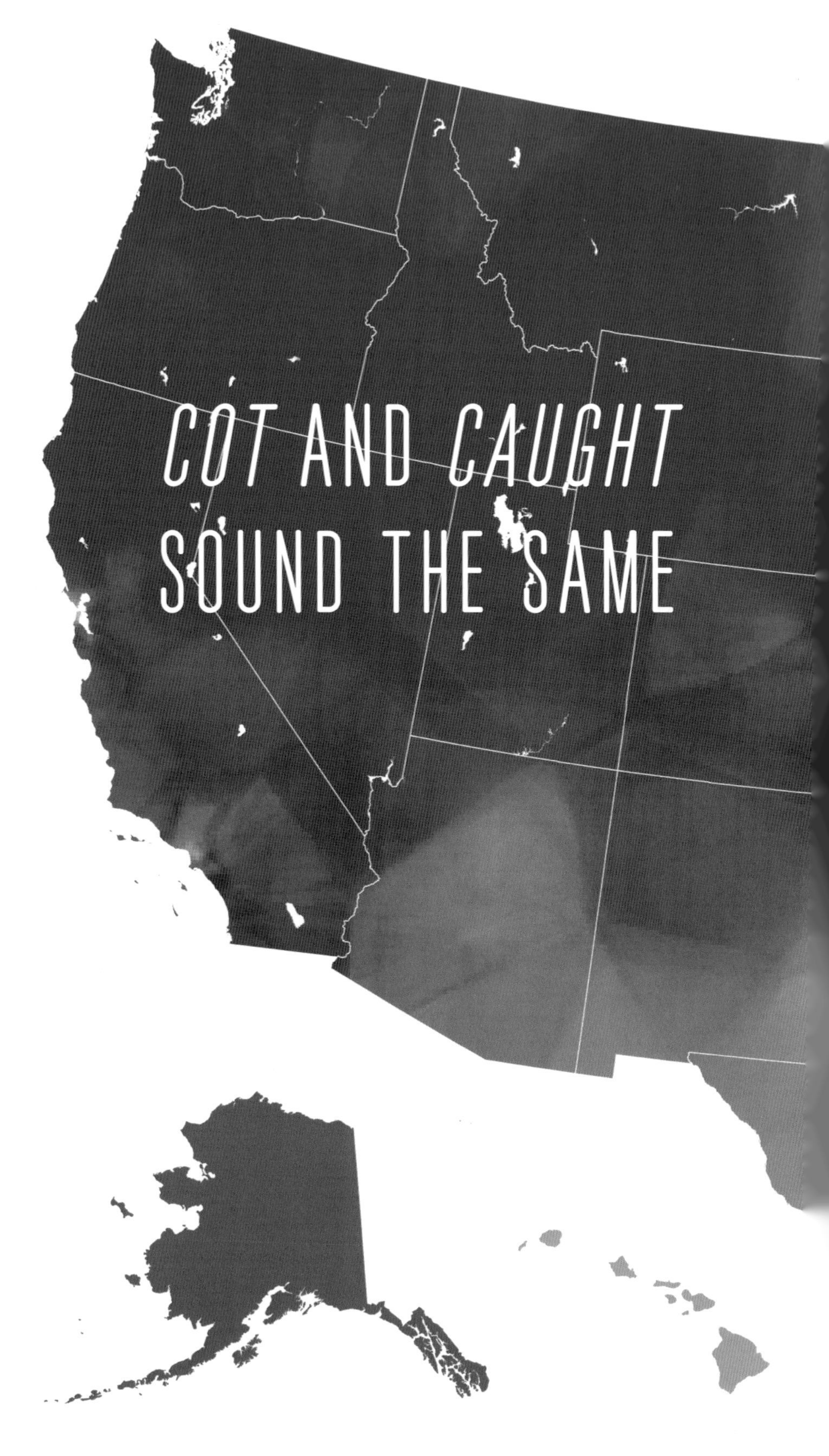

COT AND *CAUGHT*
SOUND DIFFERENT

Linguists call it a *phonemic merger:* two sounds, previously distinct, suddenly begin to slide into each other. Over time, the once separate vowel sounds become one: in this case, the short *o* sound in words like *stock, pod,* and *cot,* and the *aw* sound in words like *stalk, pawed,* and *caught*.

While we can't take a survey of 1940s American-English speakers, we can do the next best thing and see what people born in the 1940s are saying now. This lets us see the vowel merger in action, as the blue (merged) areas gradually eat away at the red (unmerged) areas among younger speakers.

Holdouts remain, and majorities in Michigan, New Jersey, New York, and Chicago continue to pronounce the words differently, but it may be a matter of time before the two sounds merge completely and American English loses a vowel sound.

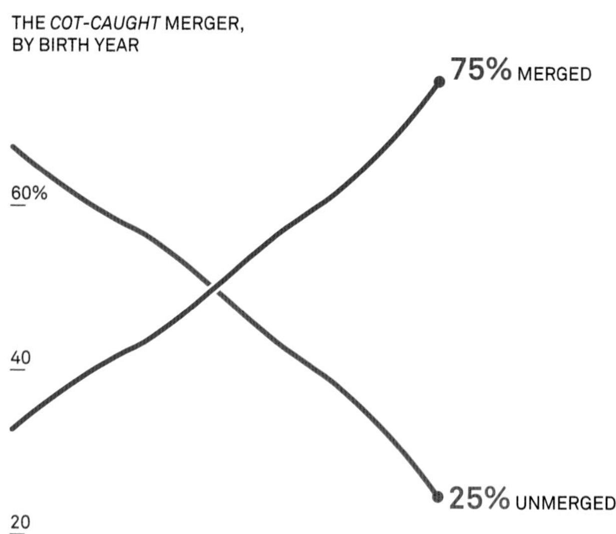

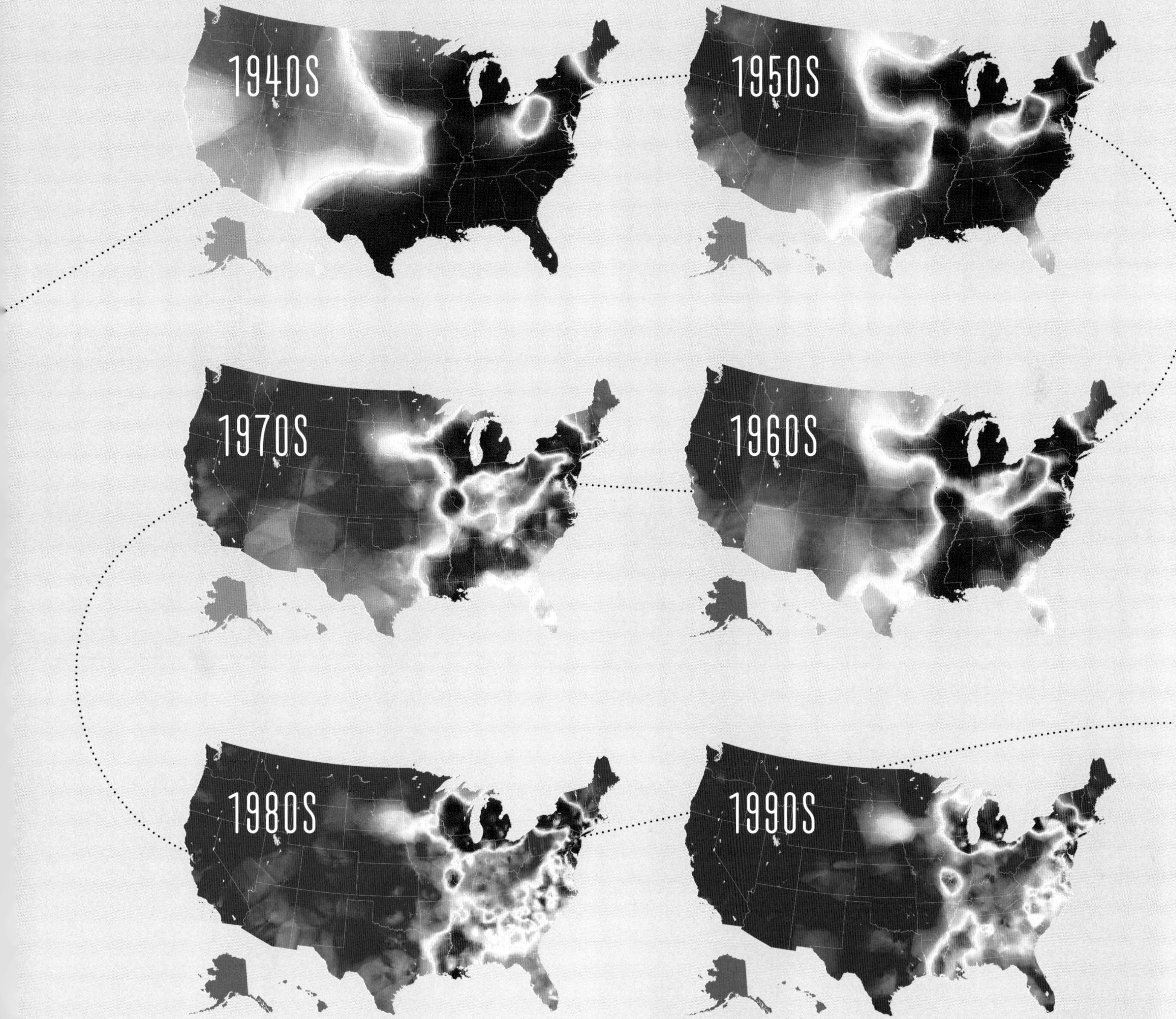

1940S

1950S

1970S

1960S

1980S

1990S

WHAT DO YOU CALL THESE?

Crayola, the marquee crayon brand from the largest crayon manufacturer in the United States, takes no official stance on the pronunciation of *crayons,* instead deferring to the dictionary, which states that "the proper way" to pronounce *crayons* is with two syllables.

KREY-AWNS 42%

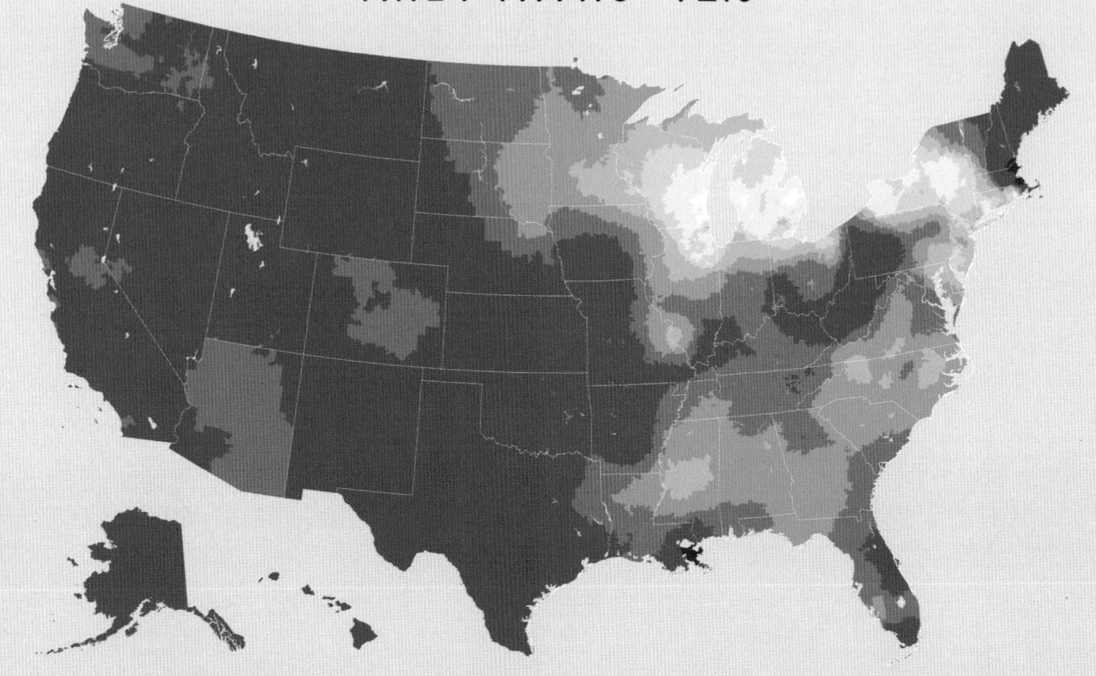

KREY-AHNS 39%

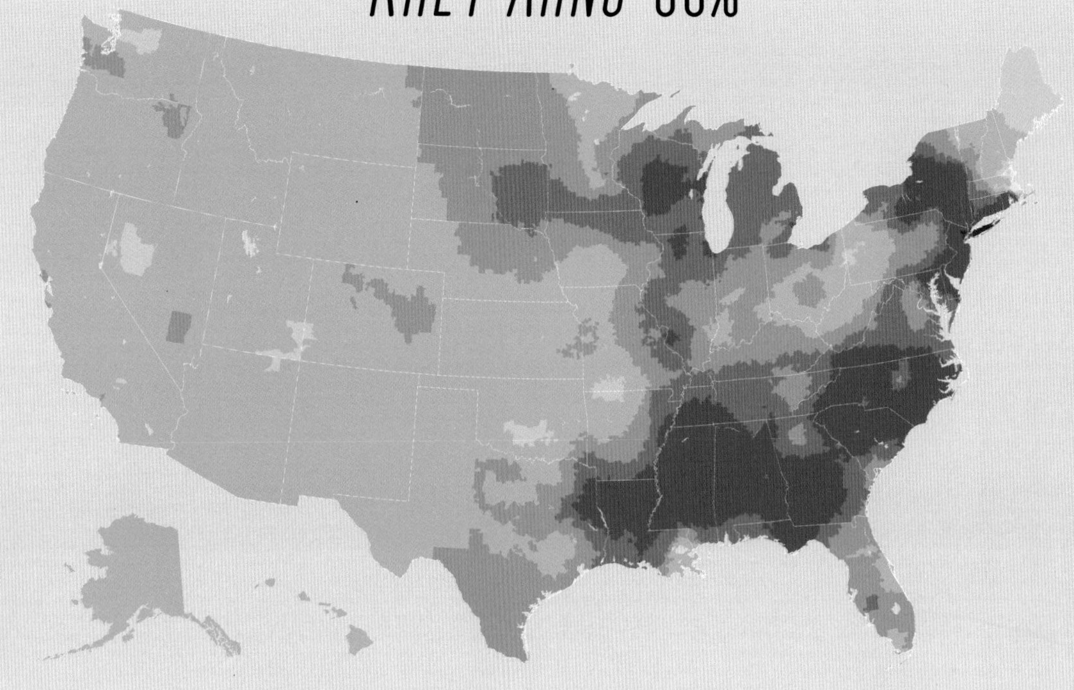

KRANS 15%

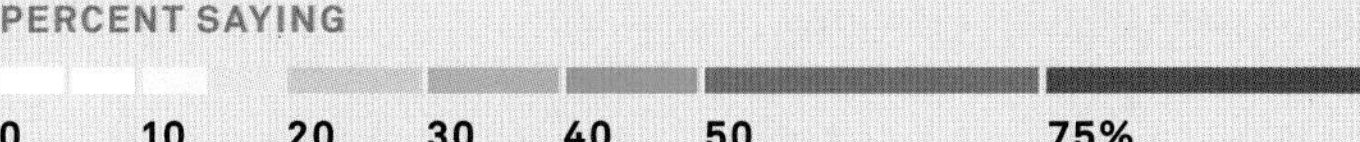

KROWNS 2%

WHAT DO YOU CALL THIS?

Though about 80 percent of the population born in 1950 pronounces the word *quarter* as though it is spelled as *kor-ter,* that pronunciation is increasingly rare. Over two-thirds of those born in the 1990s instead pronounce the word as *kwor-ter*.

PERCENT USING, BY BIRTH YEAR

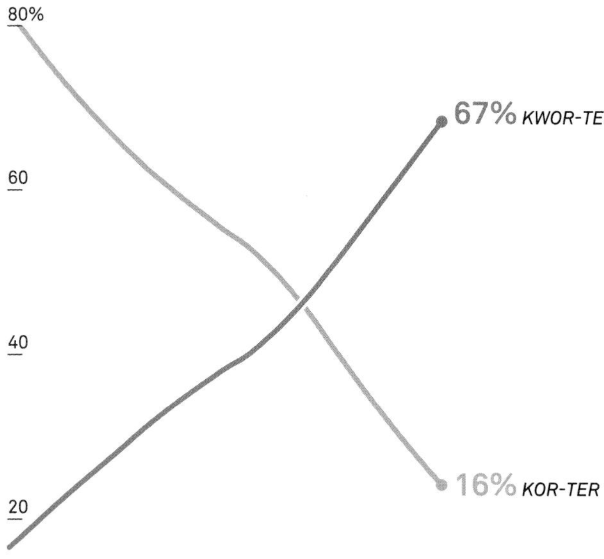

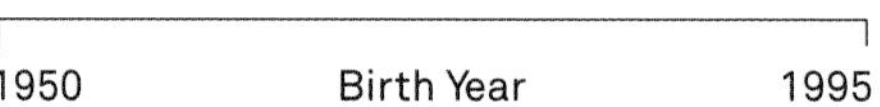

Almost 80 percent of people from both **HAWAII** and **LOUISIANA** pronounce the *w* sound and say *kwor-ter*, making for an odd geographic pairing.

PERCENT SAYING
0
10
20
30
40
50
75%
COO-PON 68%

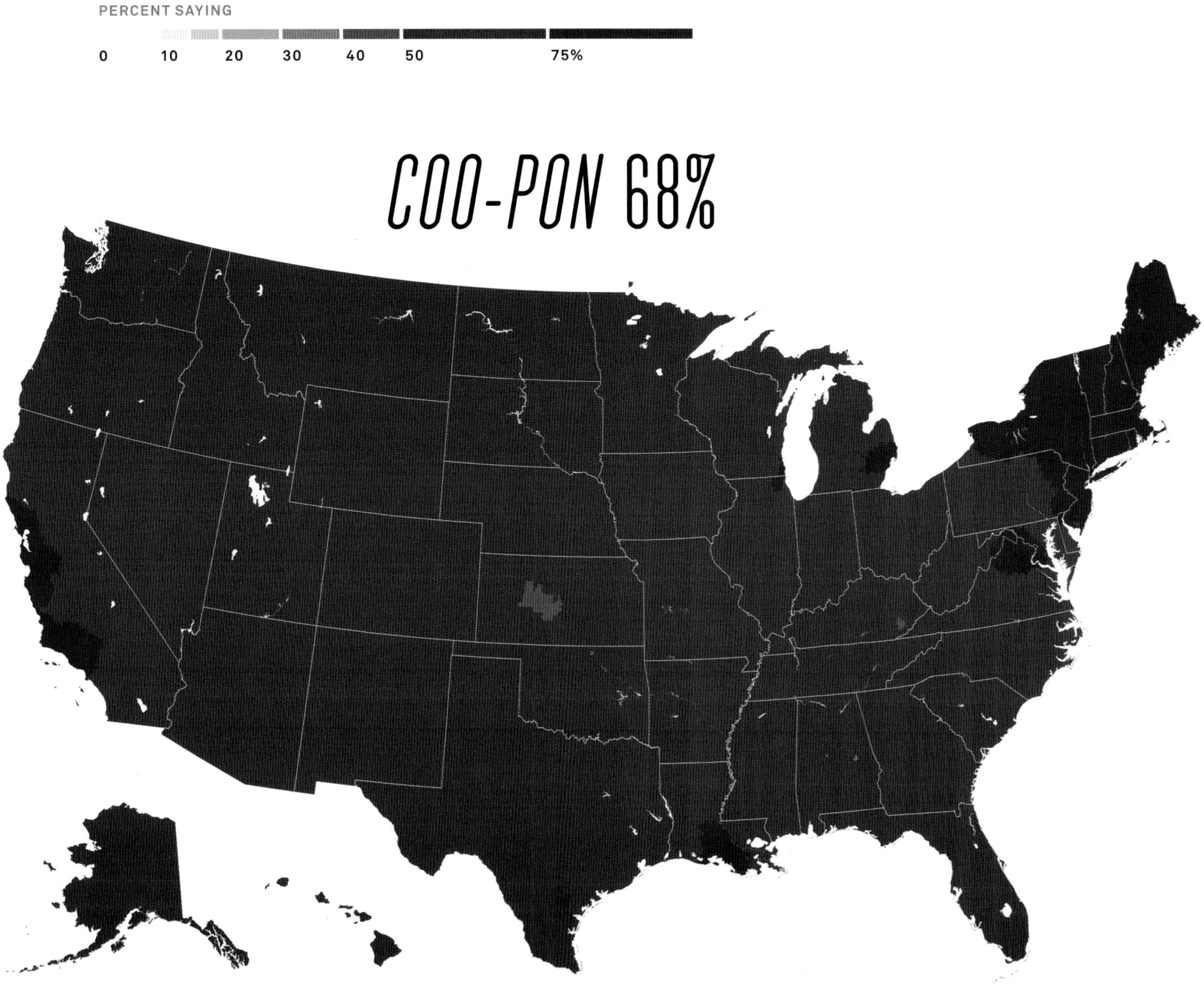

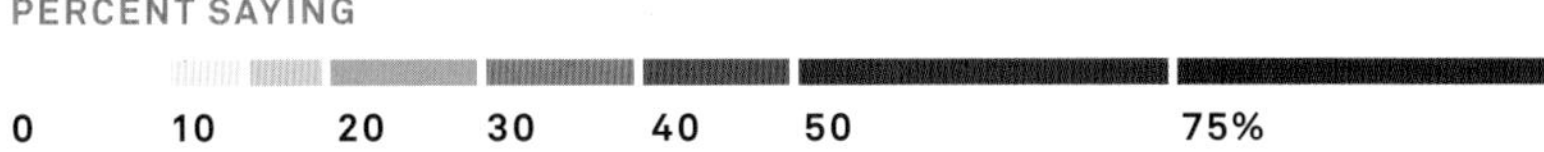

WHAT WE USE
TO SAVE MONEY

CYOO-PON 31%

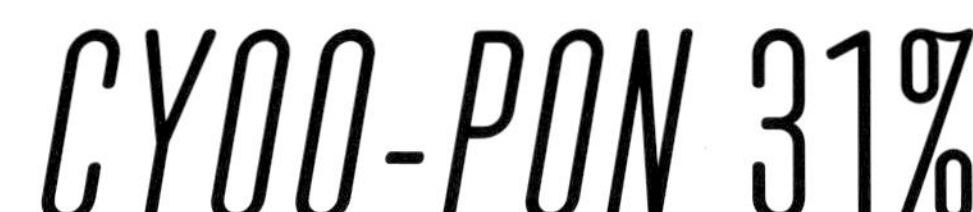

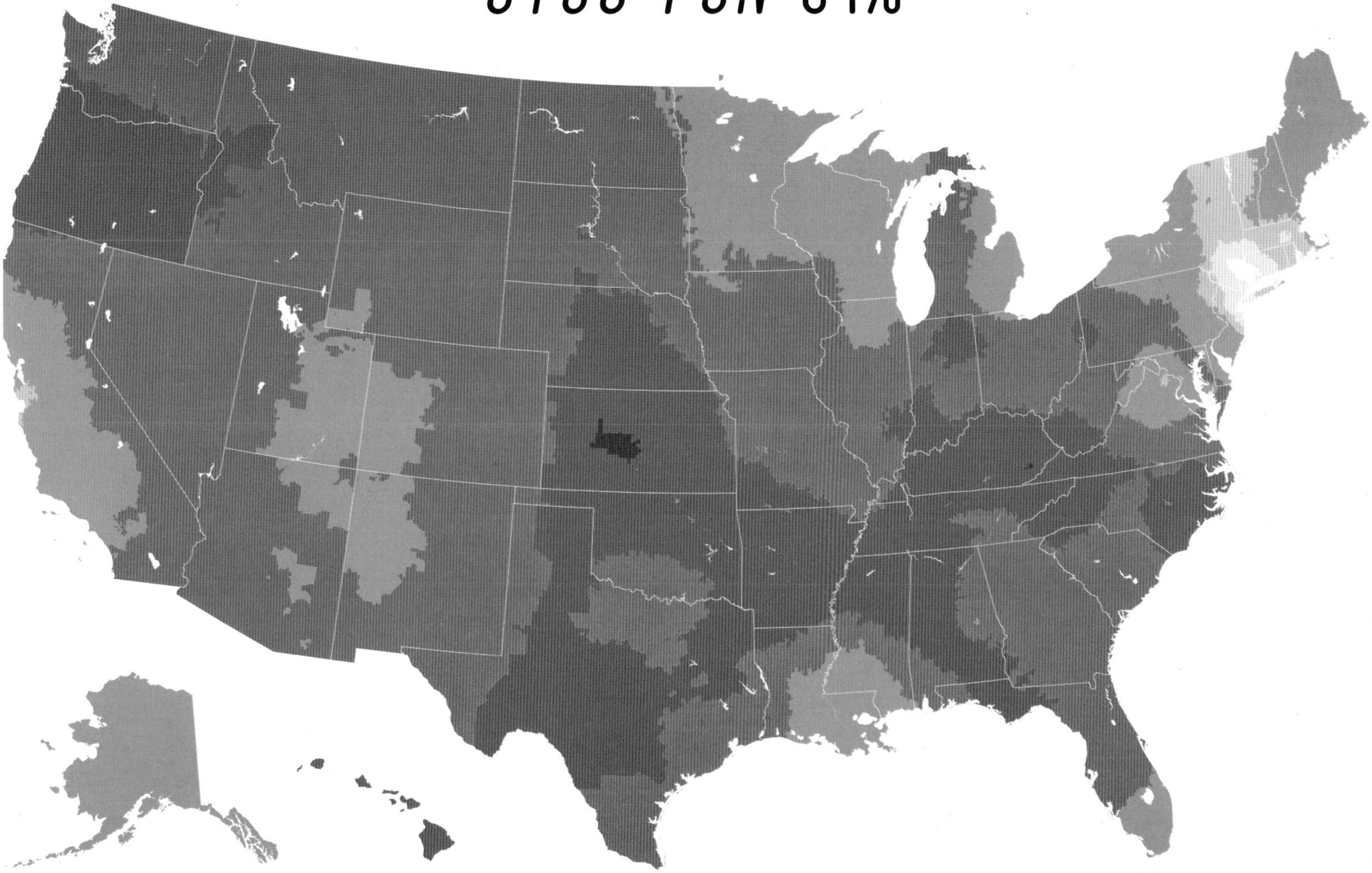

WHO TO CALL WHEN YOU GET ARRESTED

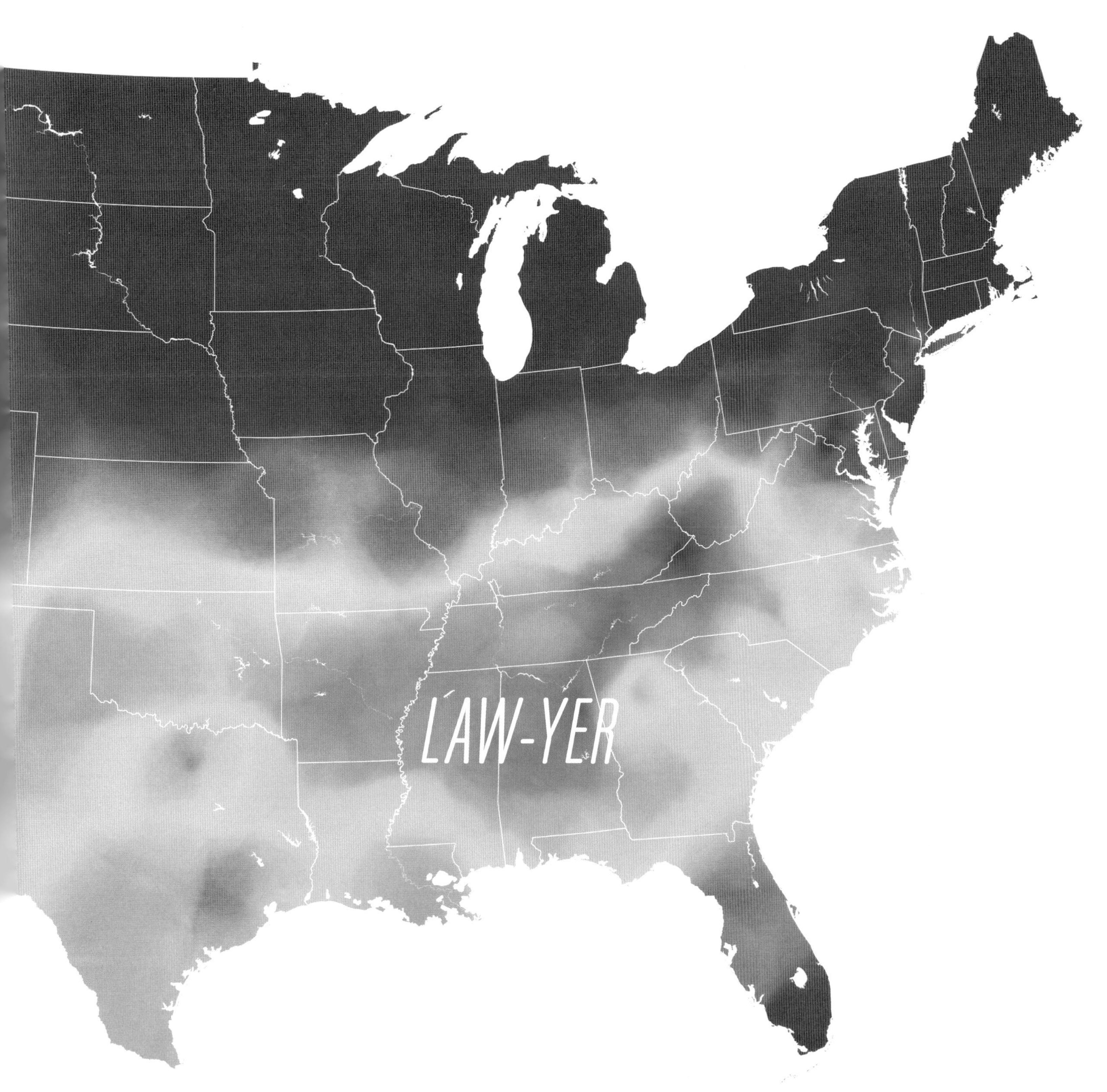
LÁW-YER

DO YOU PRONOUNCE THE FIRST *D* IN *CANDIDATE*?

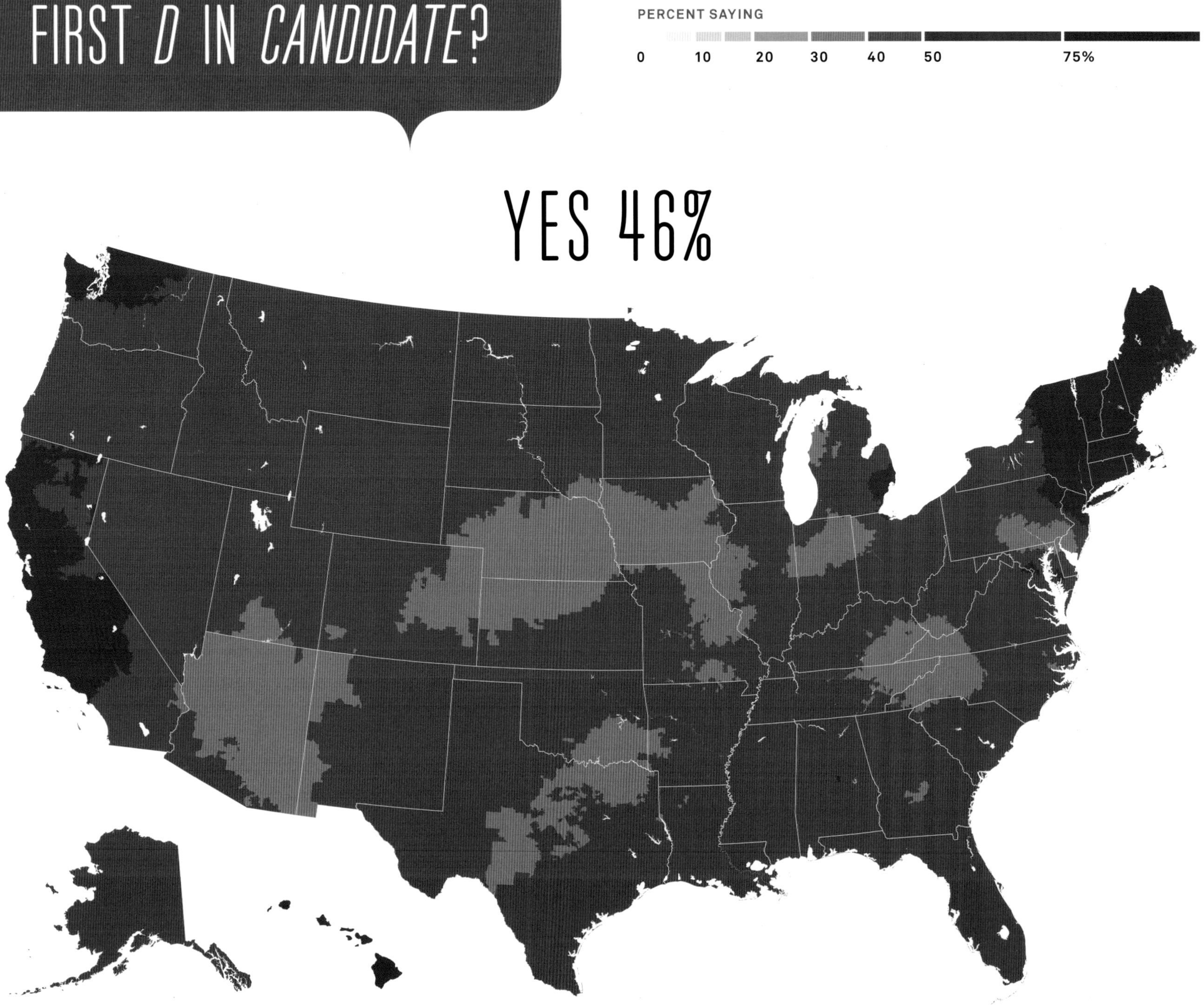

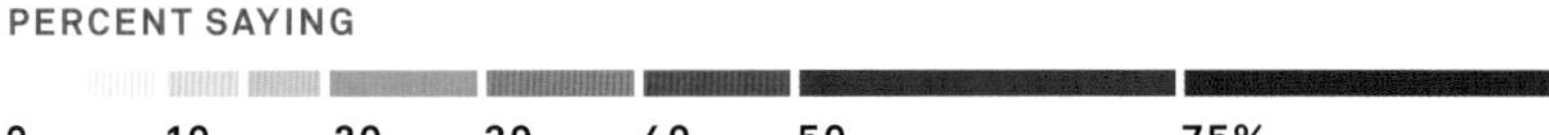

YES 46%

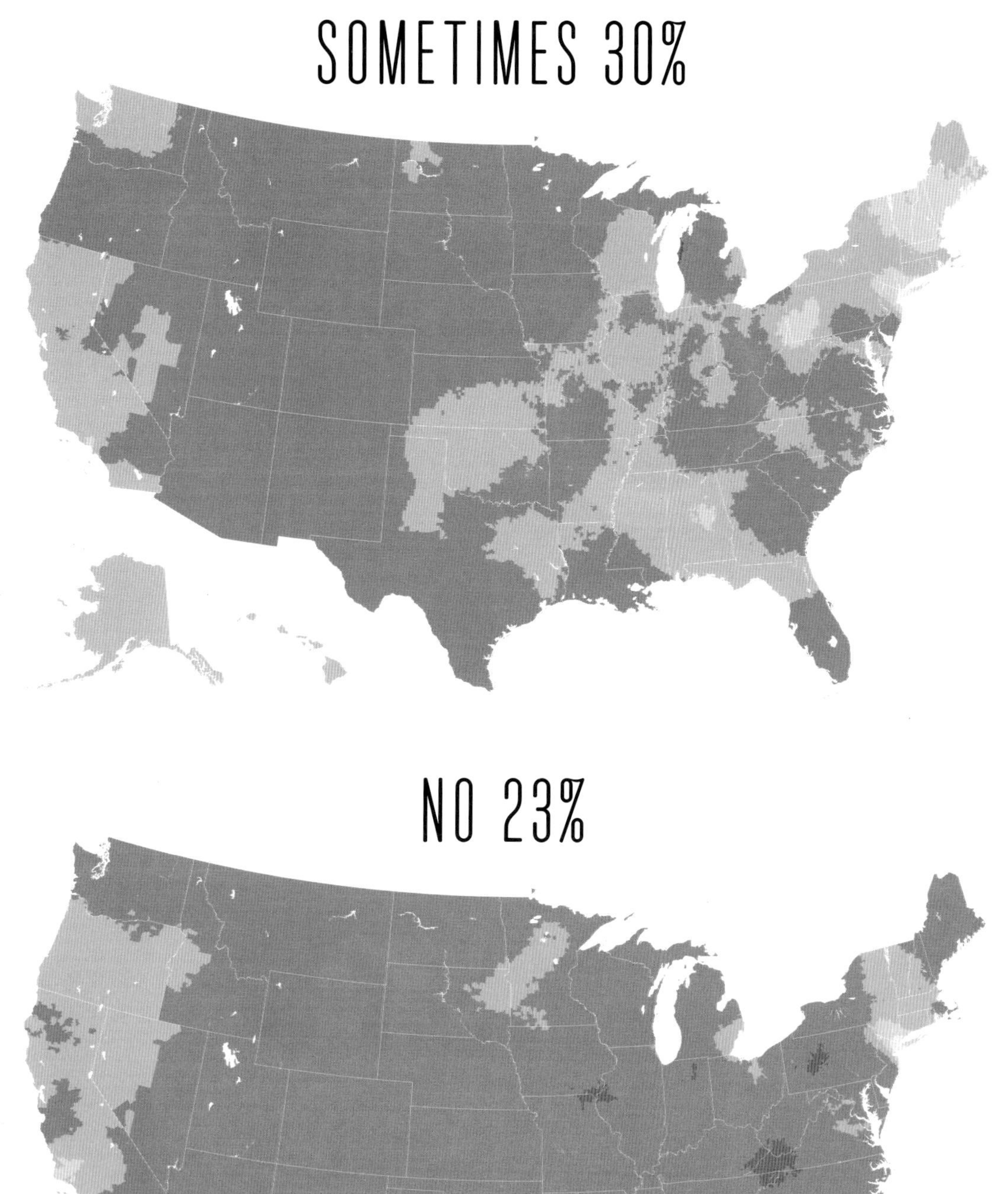
SOMETIMES 30%
NO 23%

EITHER 24%

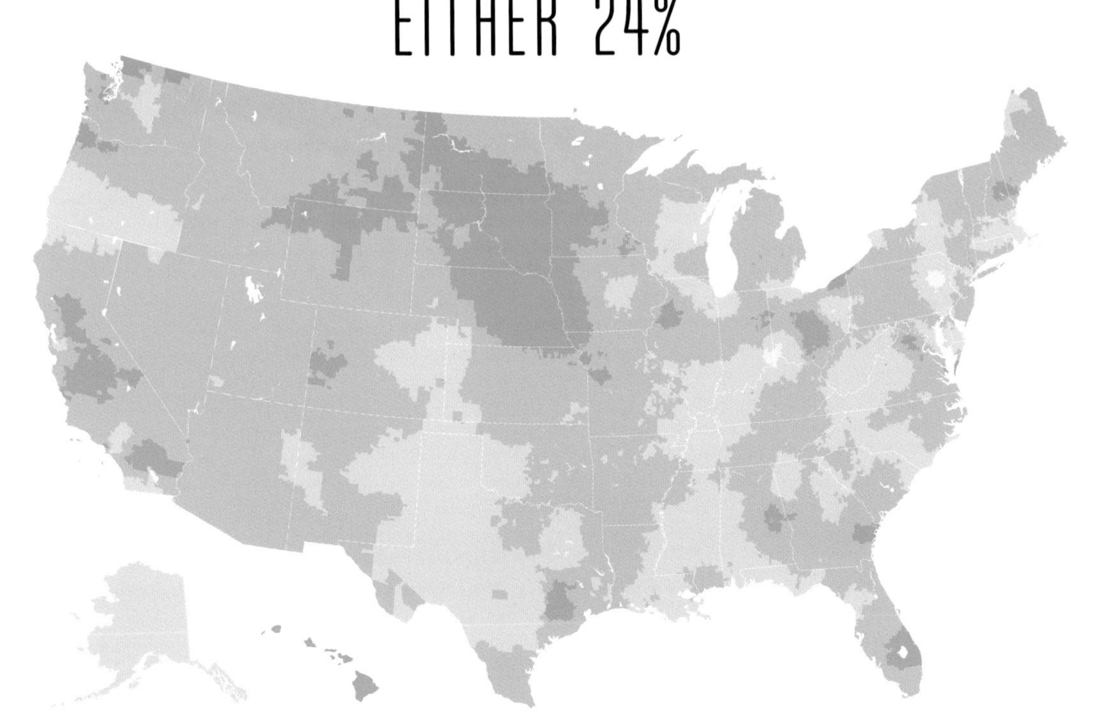

DAT-UH 23%

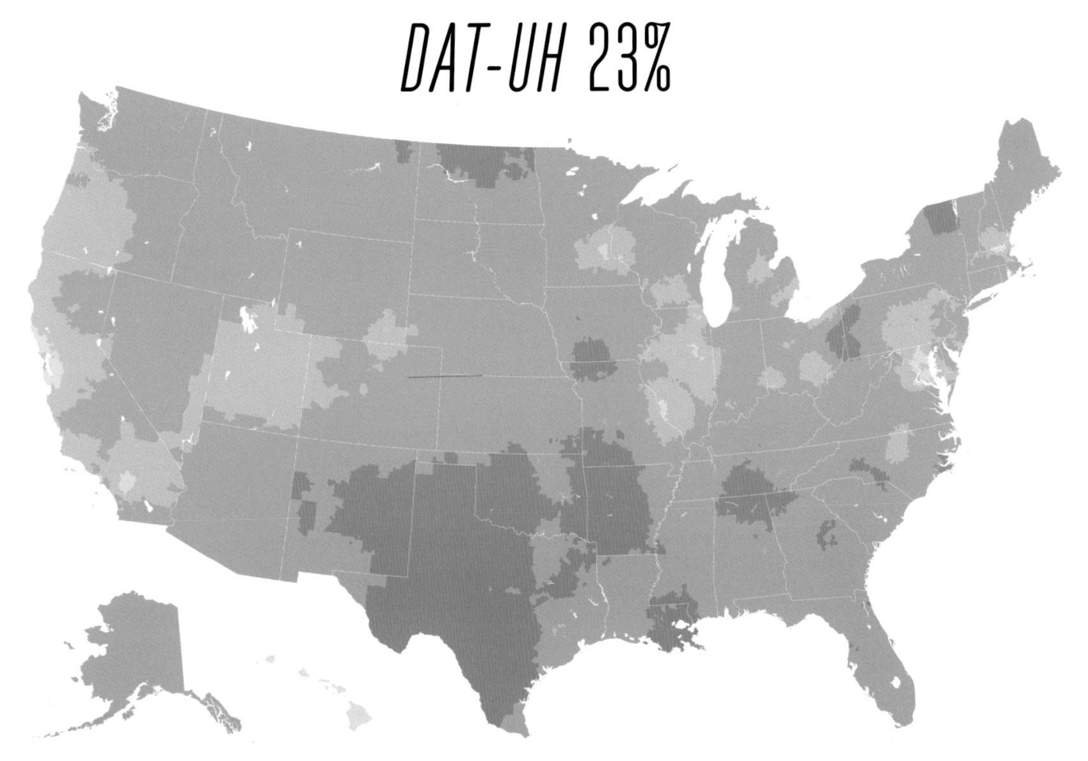

YOU SAY *DATA*. I SAY *DATA*.

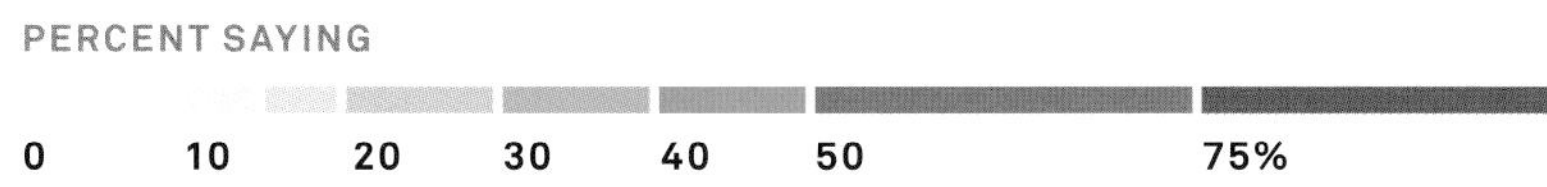

DAYT-UH 52%

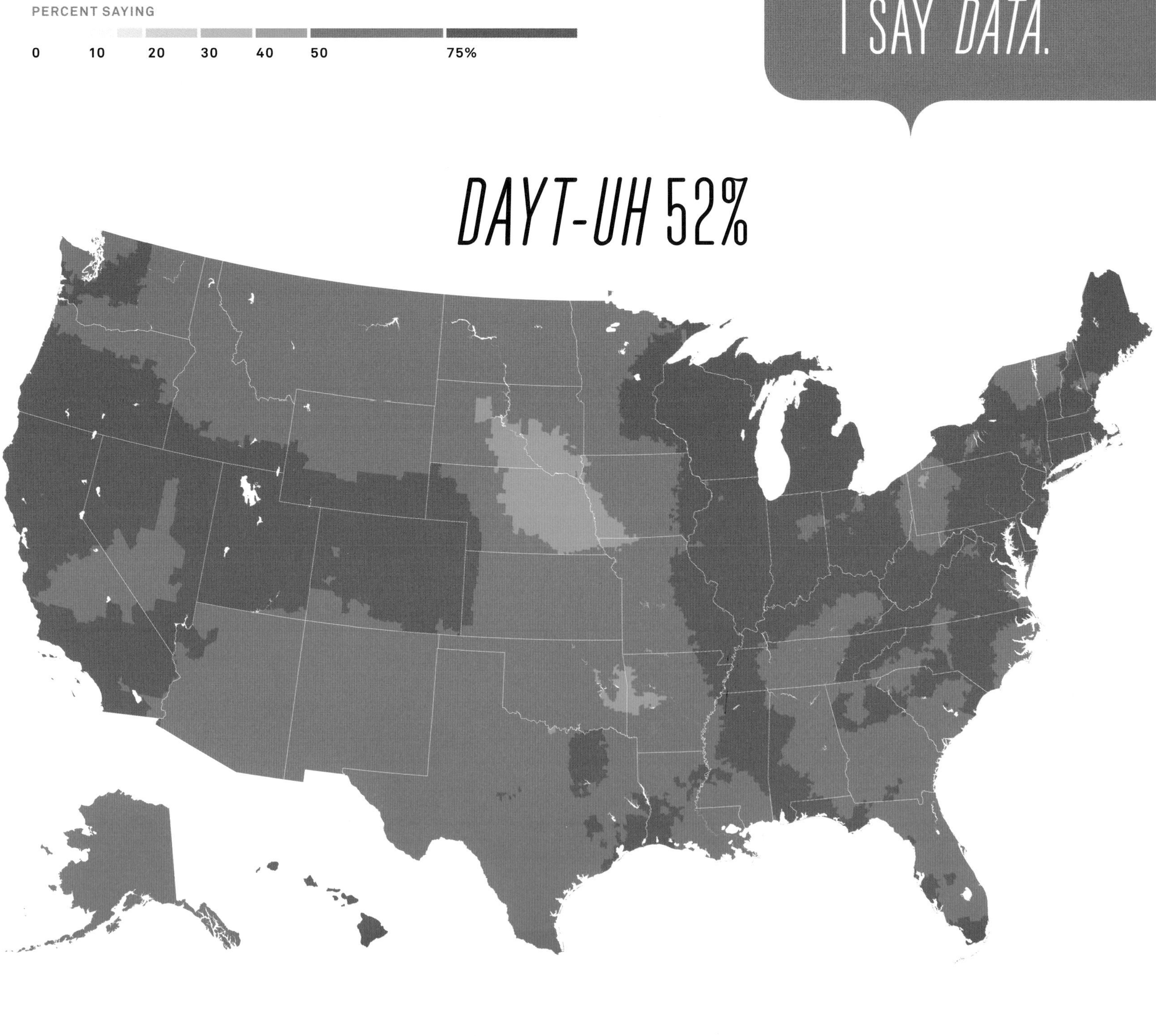

HOW WE SAY *BEEN*

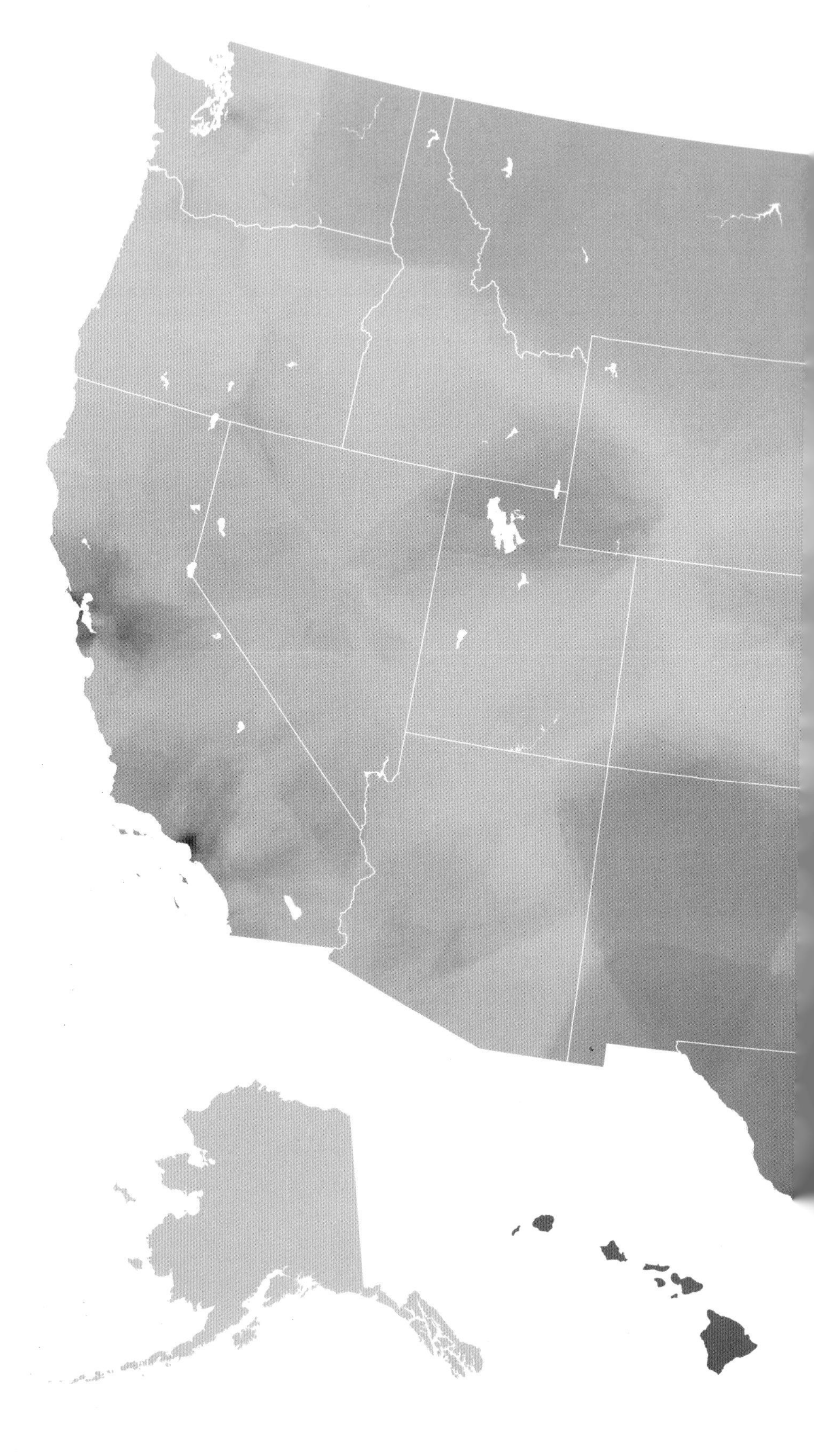

BEEN SOUNDS
LIKE *BEN*
BEEN SOUNDS
LIKE *BIN*

HOW TO PRETEND YOU'RE FROM

BOSTON

As one of the original linguistic centers of the thirteen colonies, Boston has always had its own distinct way of speaking. The phrase "Park your car in Harvard Yard"—or, for the Bostonian, "*Pahk ya cah in Havad Yahd*"—has become the standard cliché to test for a Boston accent. But the prevalence of that accent, particularly the Boston Brahmin accent of the old Boston upper class, has lessened over time. While the dropped *r* for which Boston has long been known is not as widespread as it once was, New England has an entire vocabulary of its own.

Here, you might *hosey* (claim) the front seat of the car on the way to the town *common*. What elsewhere would be a *milk shake* roughly half the people in New England call a *frappe* (in Rhode Island it's a *cabinet*), and almost 8 percent of people call soda *tonic*. You might hear a shopping cart called a *carriage* and, especially in Vermont, a mountain lion called a *catamount*. And, as we've seen, Rhode Island is one of the few places outside of Wisconsin where you're likely to hear a water fountain called a *bubbler,* with or without the *r*.

HOW TO PRETEND YOU'RE FROM

WESTERN NEW ENGLAND

Western New England, the region squeezed between the linguistic centers of Boston to the east and New York to the west, has developed its own way of speaking that is distinct from both. Here you'll find *tag sales* and *grinders,* and you get your water from a *drinking fountain* rather than a *water fountain* (or a *bubbler,* as you would in Rhode Island to the east). In Connecticut, the night before Halloween is *Mischief Night;* in Vermont it's *Cabbage Night*.

HOW TO PRETEND YOU'RE FROM

BALTIMORE

Dialect-wise, Maryland is an odd state. It lies south of the Mason-Dixon Line, but in style is a northeastern city, part of the megalopolis stretching from Washington, D.C., up to Boston.

Where New York has *stoops,* Baltimore (pronounced *Bawlmer*) has *front steps*. While you're there, head *down the ocean* and pick up some *carry-out: coddies* (deep-fried potato cakes flavored with salt cod), a *chicken box* (carry-out consisting of a box of fried chicken and french fries), *half-and-half* (a drink of half sweet tea, half lemonade), a *snoball* (shaved ice doused in a sweet syrup, served in a Styrofoam cup), and *lake trout* (battered and fried whiting, usually served with white bread and hot sauce). Then wash it all down with a six-pack of *Natty Boh*. (That's National Bohemian beer, formerly brewed in Baltimore, now owned by Pabst Brewing Company in Los Angeles. Incidentally, Pabst was the first American brewer to sell cans of beer in six-packs.)

And Baltimore's probably the last place in the country you might still see *arabbers* (pronounced *ay-rabber,* the first syllable rhyming with *day*) on the streets—men selling produce from horse-drawn carts.

Arabbing was one plentiful in the city but has been in decline since around World War II. While today only a handful of arabbers remain on the streets of Baltimore, the practice has a history stretching back to the years immediately after the Civil War. Maryland was a border state during the war—a slave state that fought for the North—hence it was not covered by the Emancipation Proclamation. After slavery was abolished in Maryland in 1864, arabbing was one of the few jobs available for black men, and it developed into a tradition, a business that was often passed down from fathers to sons.

HOW TO PRETEND YOU'RE FROM

NEW YORK

One of the most distinct dialects in the public imagination is that of New York—or, that is, *Noo Yawk*. Among other things, the stereotypical New York accent often drops the *h* in *huge* in favor of a *y,* so the word sounds like *yuge*. Like accents in Boston and parts of the Deep South, it is nonrhotic—dropping the *r* sound unless it is followed by a vowel, so that *butter* becomes *buttah* and *card* becomes *cahd*. For a long time, people considered this to be a mark of refinement. Think Franklin Delano Roosevelt. But over time, as with many strong accent markers, Americans began to associate nonrhotic speech with the working class, and it began to fade away.

But while accent becomes a marker of class, broader dialect signals, particularly those involving word choice, are generally more subtle. Regional words for common nouns are typically less tied to education and economic levels and are not consciously suppressed (of course there are exceptions to this rule, as anyone who has ordered a *pop* in the Northeast can tell you).

For one thing, New Yorkers almost always wait *on line,* not *in line*. When you get to the head of the line, the cashier may ask for the *following guest* to step down, a relatively new development that's taken hold only over the past twenty years or so. Around New York, especially in the outer boroughs and Long Island, you might order a *hero* rather than a *sub* and then take it back to your *walk-up* (an apartment in a building that doesn't have an elevator).

Of course, all of this really applies to New York City, Long Island, and the northern half of New Jersey. The rest of New York—that is, *upstate*—is an entirely different story. The eastern portion of the state is, linguistically, more a part of Connecticut, Vermont, and western New England. The western part—Buffalo, Rochester, and Syracuse—is its own dialect region.

As you drive west along the New York State Thruway and into upstate New York, you're actually passing from the northeastern coastal dialect regions into a wholly different place, linguistically: the region linguists refer to as the Inland North—a stretch of counties running along the southern shores of the Great Lakes, from Buffalo to Cleveland, through southern Michigan to northern Illinois and Milwaukee.

It's here you find a vowel pattern that linguist William Labov dubbed the Northern Cities Shift, a series of changes in vowel sounds that researchers first noted in the 1960s. Linguists often think of vowels in terms of the position of the speaker's tongue. You probably don't think about this much while you're speaking, but the different vowel sounds come about largely from having your tongue in various positions in your mouth.

Suppose that you and everyone you speak to start to change the way you pronounce a vowel. Say that your short *a* starts becoming "raised" and "fronted" (meaning that your tongue is higher and more forward in your mouth) so that *cat* starts to sound more like *kit*. But before your tongue gets too far, it ends up back where it started, turning the vowel into a diphthong (a syllable with two vowel sounds): *kyat*. As the short *a* changes position, pretty soon it's running into the space where the short *i* sound usually is. Sometimes when this happens, the sounds merge. But if the two sounds are to remain distinct, the short *i* has to go somewhere else, which it does, moving toward a short *u,* making *bit* sound like *but*. Then the short *u* moves toward the *aw* sound in words like *straw*.

This picture of the Northern Cities Shift is, of course, an oversimplified description. Rather than the dynamic described above where one vowel "pushes" another out of the way, linguists generally believe that the process is more akin to a "pull," where vowels move to occupy the space vacated by other shifted vowels.

Only some of these shifts have occurred throughout the Inland North, but you can hear examples of each to some extent in various combinations throughout the region.

HOW TO PRETEND YOU'RE FROM

CHICAGO

Lace up your *gym shoes* and head to Chicago, where you don't ride the subway but the *L,* the elevated rapid transit system whose tracks crisscross the city (analogous to the *T* in Boston). Even the sections of track that are underground are still referred to as the *L,* which you might take to avoid the *gapers' block* or *gapers' delay* (a traffic jam caused by drivers staring at an accident) on the *expressway.*

Overall, if you say *gapers' block, expressway,* and *gym shoes,* there's a greater than 95 percent chance you're from the Chicago area.

4

Part Four

WHERE WE GO

WHAT WE CALL

A FREIGHT TRUCK

Elsewhere in the English-speaking world, you might find a *transport truck* (Canada) or an *articulated lorry* (Ireland and the United Kingdom), but in the United States, depending on where you are, you're likely to see a *semi* (or *semi-truck*), a *tractor-trailer,* or an *eighteen-wheeler.*

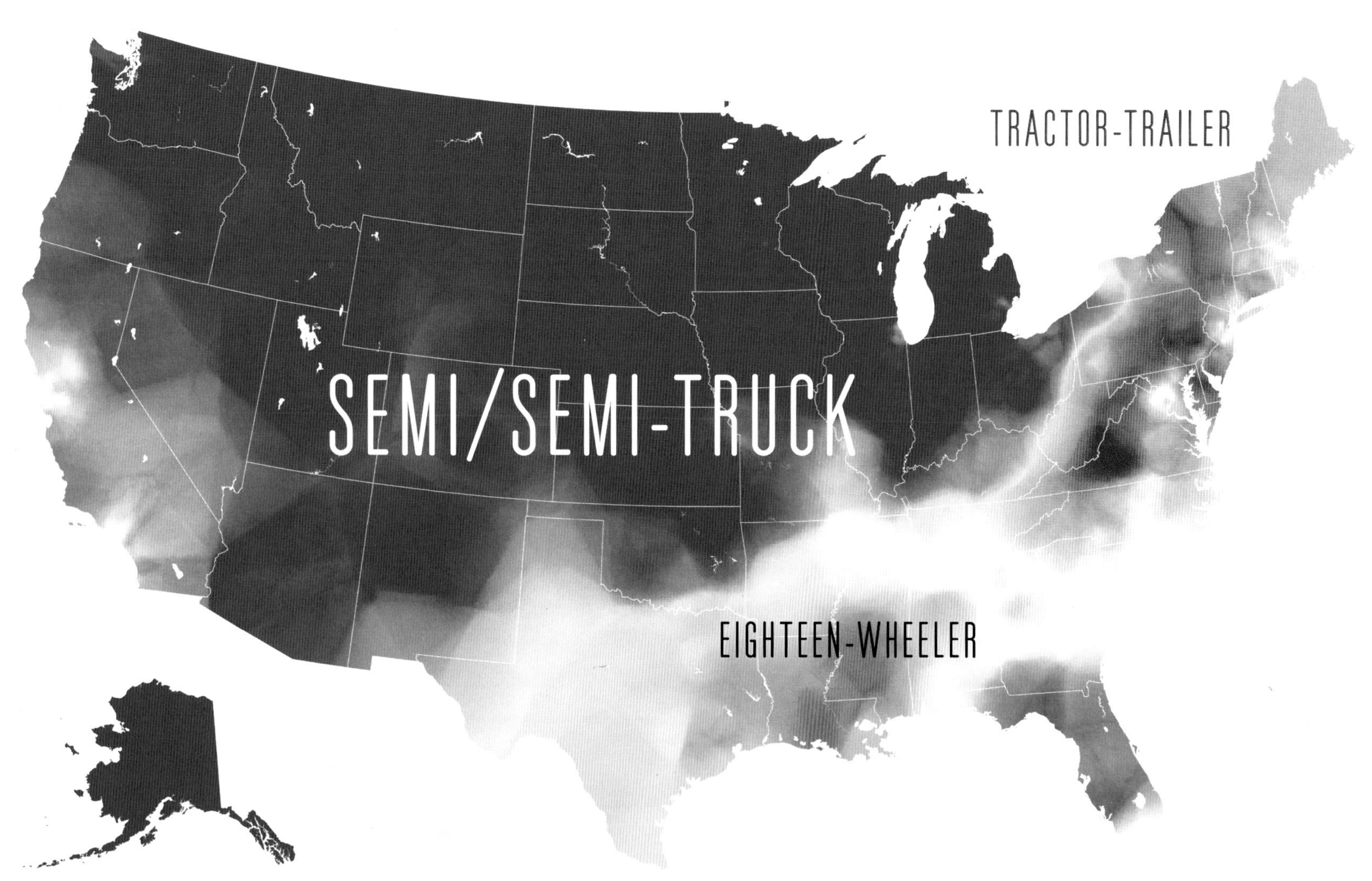

Not particularly common anywhere, but almost unheard-of outside of **CALIFORNIA**, a *rig* or *big rig* is most common around **SACRAMENTO**, **SAN FRANCISCO**, and parts of **LOS ANGELES**.

RIG/BIG RIG

PERCENT SAYING *RIG/BIG RIG*

0 5 10 15 20 >25%

WHAT WE SAY WHEN WE WANT OUR FRIENDS TO JOIN US

People are most likely to ask "You coming with?" in Minnesota and Chicago, but language divisions are not only geographic.

Regardless of where you live, the younger you are, the more likely you are to ask "You coming with?" as a complete sentence. Fewer than 20 percent of Americans born in 1950 do so, compared to half of those born in 1995 or later.

PERCENT ASKING "YOU COMING WITH?", BY BIRTH YEAR

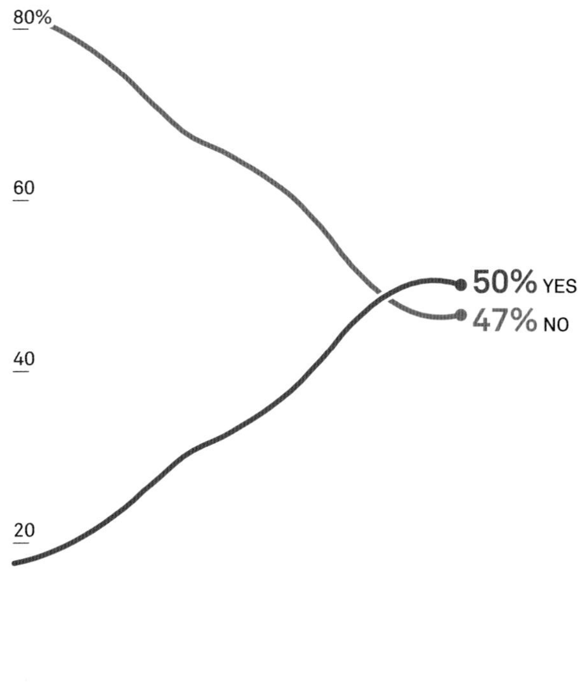

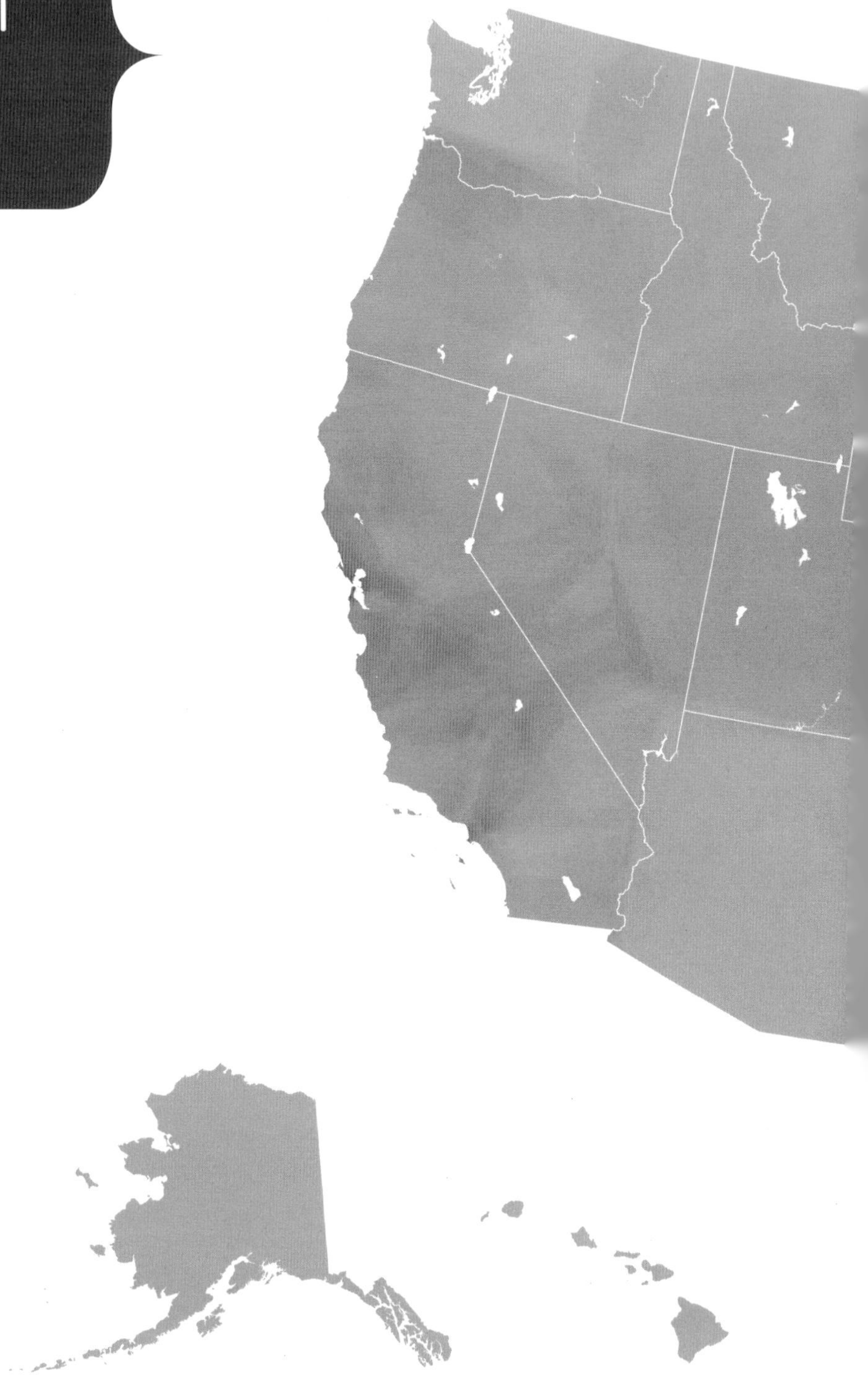

WHERE THEY ASK
"YOU COMING WITH?"
WHERE THEY DON'T

HOW WE SAY *ROUTE*

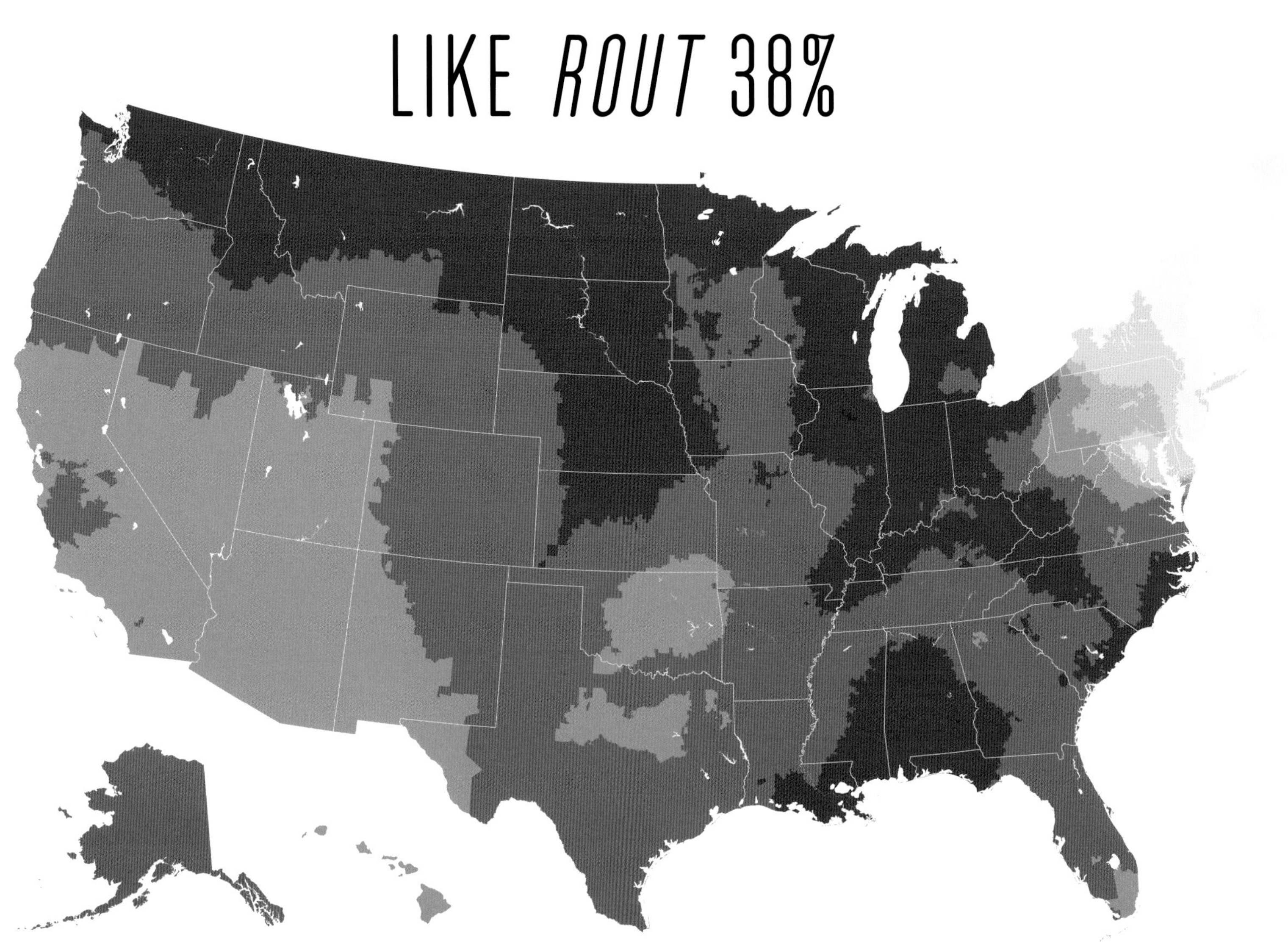

PERCENT SAYING *ROUTE*
0
10
20
30
40
50
75%
LIKE *ROOT* 39%

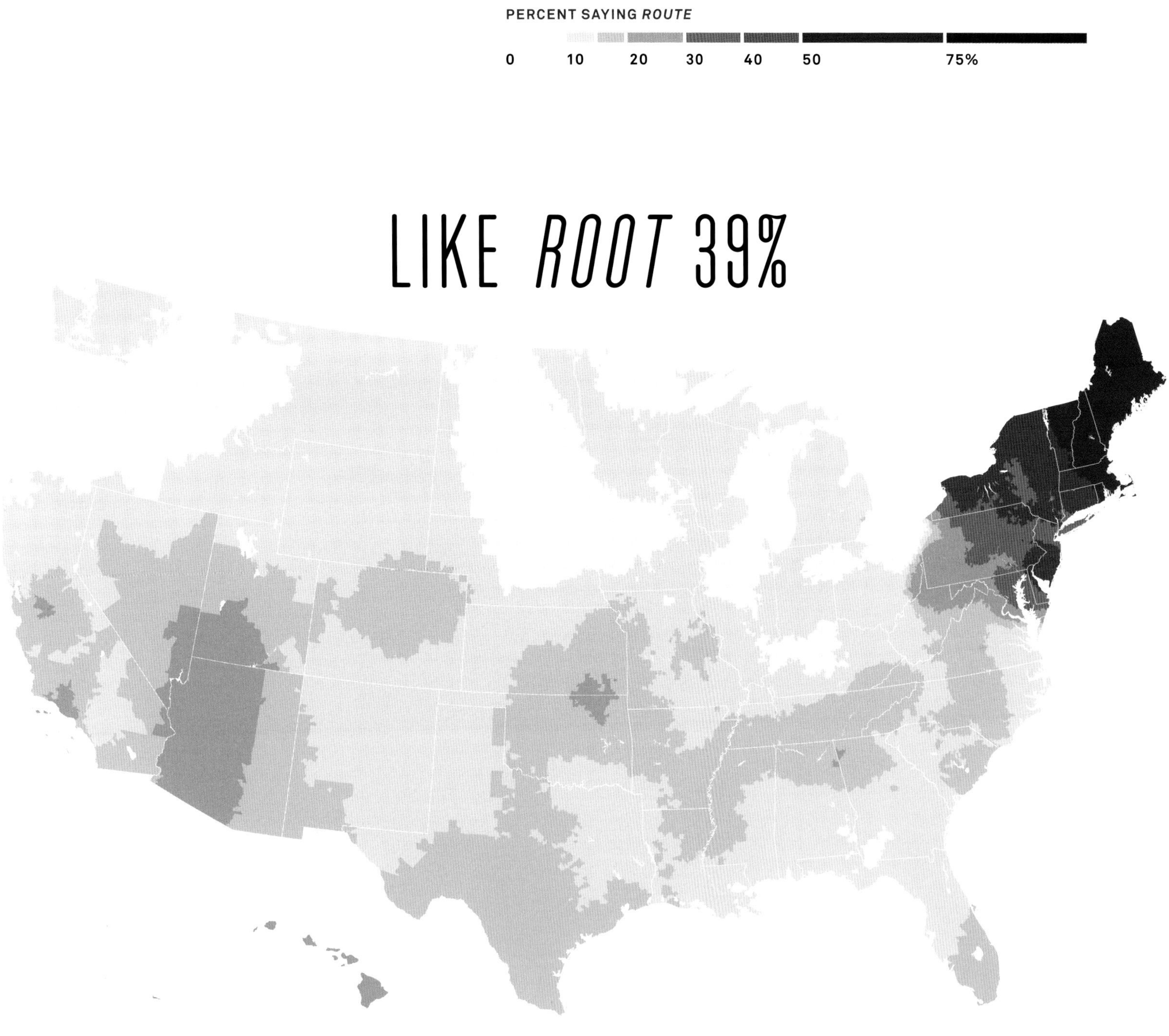

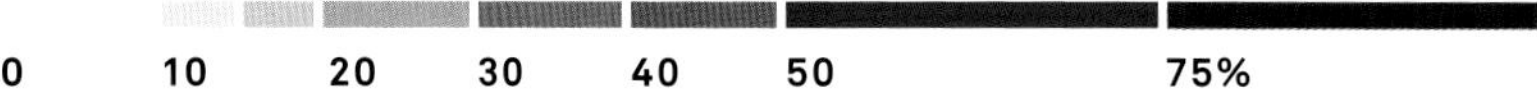

WHAT WE DRIVE ON

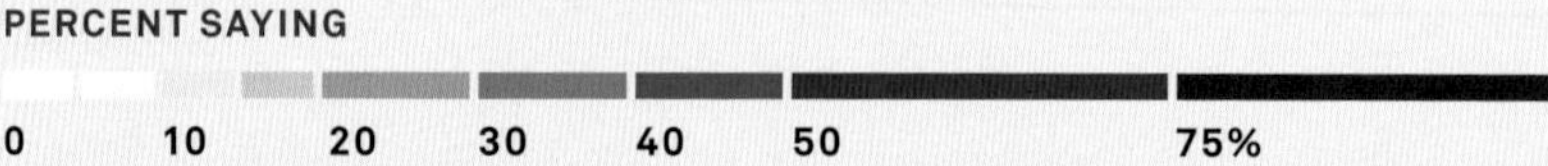

HIGHWAY 56%

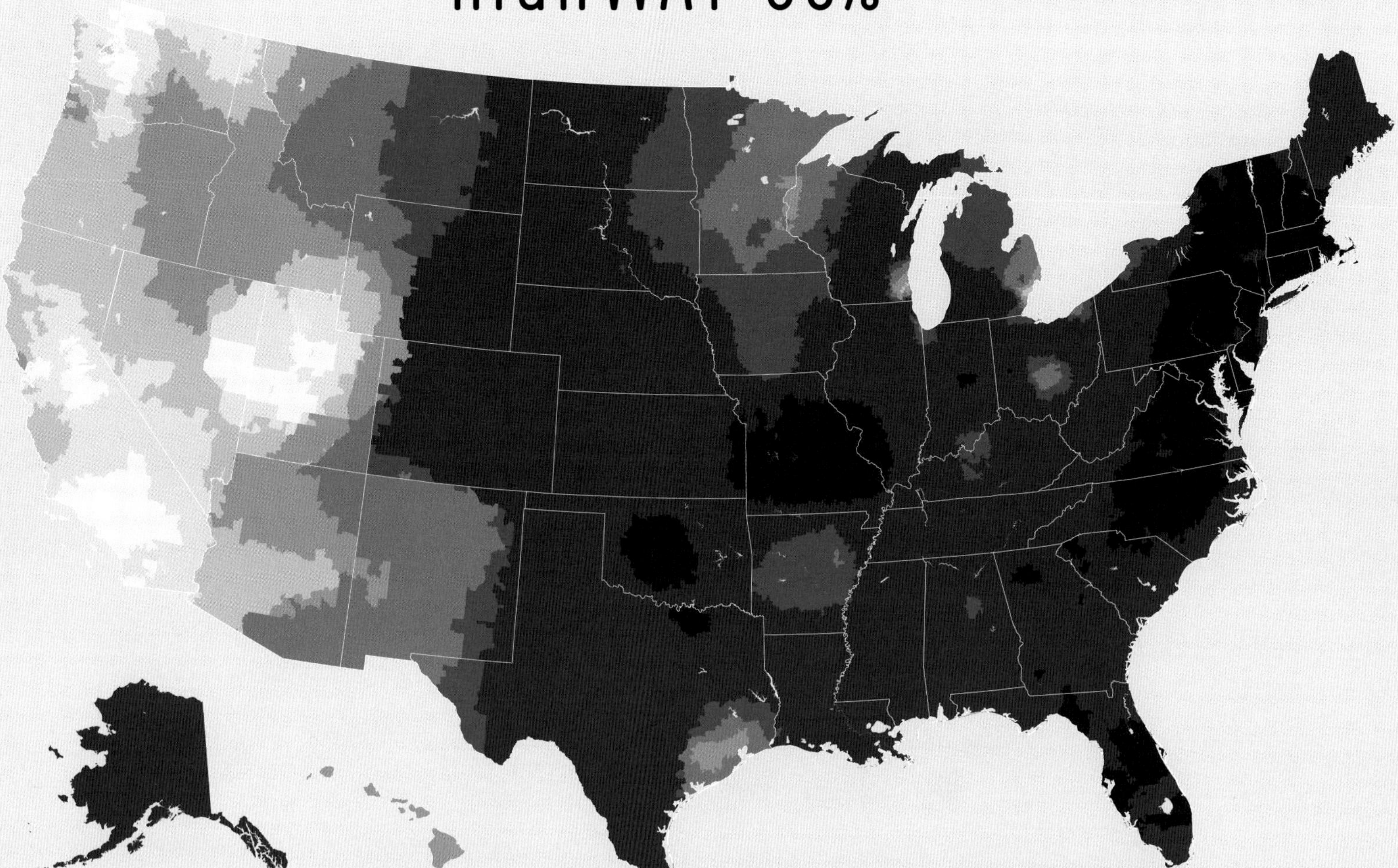

FREEWAY 31%

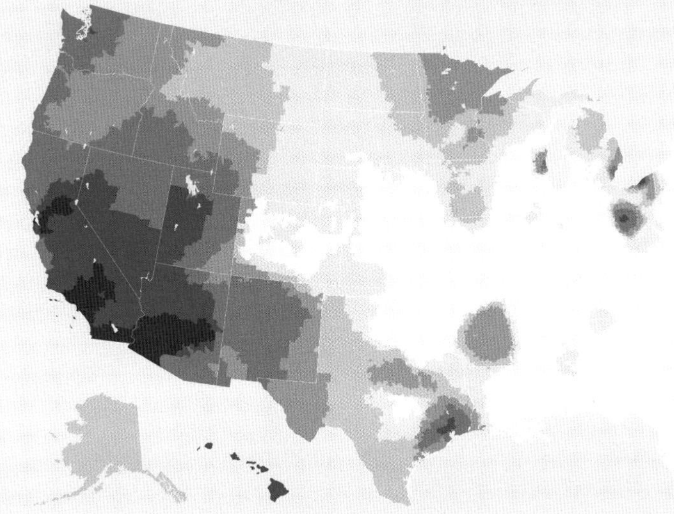

EXPRESSWAY 4%

THRUWAY <1%

A very clear dividing line between **BUFFALO** and **ROCHESTER**, **NEW YORK**, emerges once you start asking people about their generic word for *highway*. In **BUFFALO**, whose suburbs the New York State Thruway cuts through on its way south, over a third of people use *thruway* as their generic term, the highest percentage in the country by far. Nowhere else in the United States has a percentage higher than 10.

In **ROCHESTER**, on the other hand, with its Eastern and Western Expressways, you're more likely to encounter *expressway* than anywhere else in the country outside of **CHICAGO**, **ILLINOIS**, and **FLINT**, **MICHIGAN**.

FRONTAGE ROAD 31%

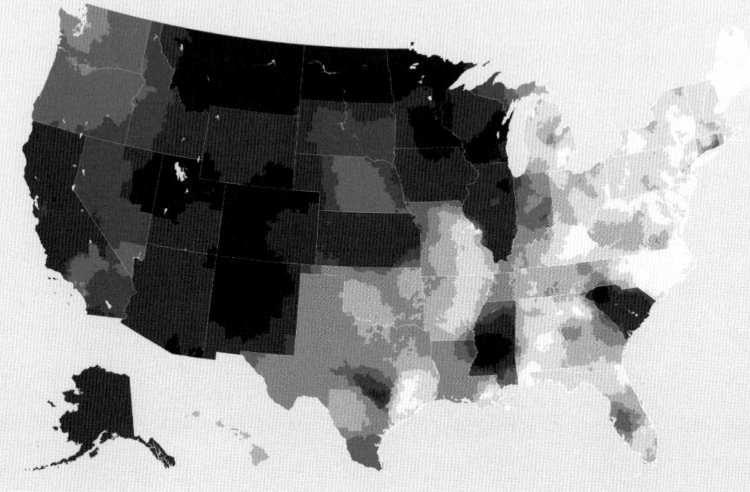

SERVICE ROAD 26%

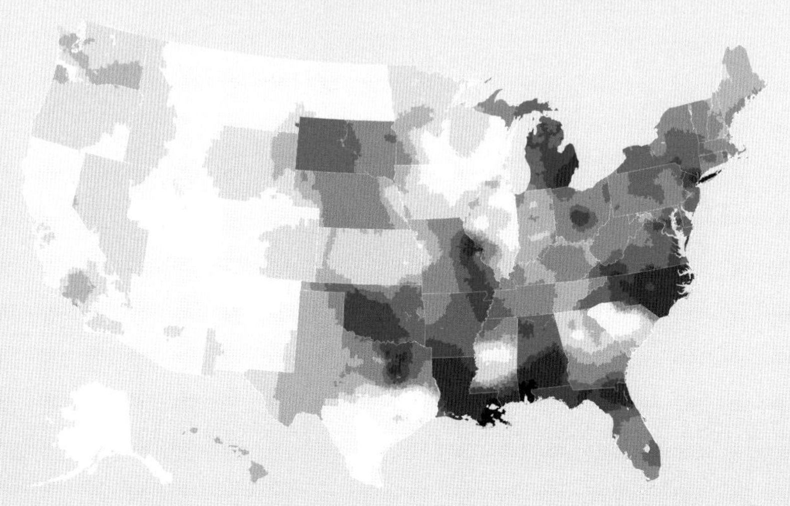

ACCESS ROAD 20%

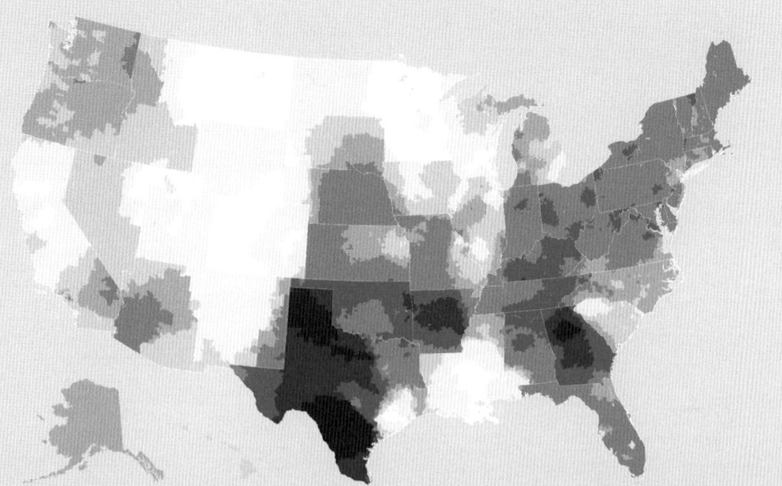

NO WORD FOR THIS 18%

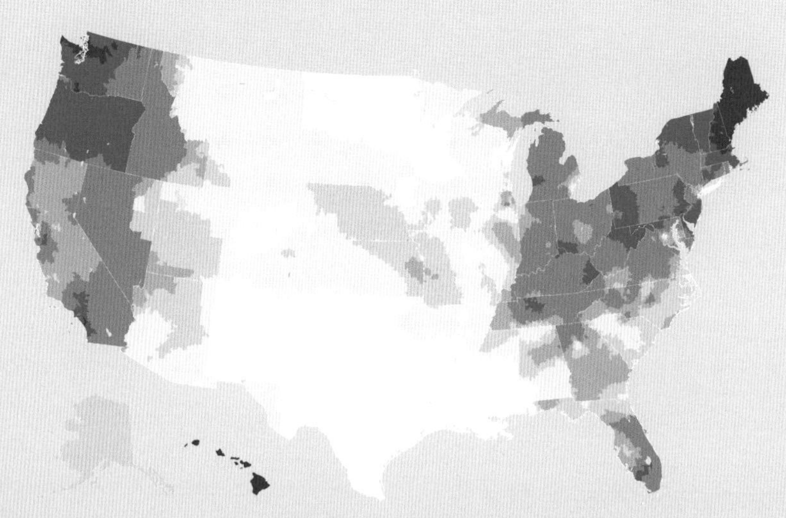

FEEDER ROAD 3%

WHAT WE CALL THE LITTLE ROAD THAT RUNS ALONGSIDE THE HIGHWAY

OUTER ROAD <1%

PERCENT SAYING

0 10 20 30 40 50 75%

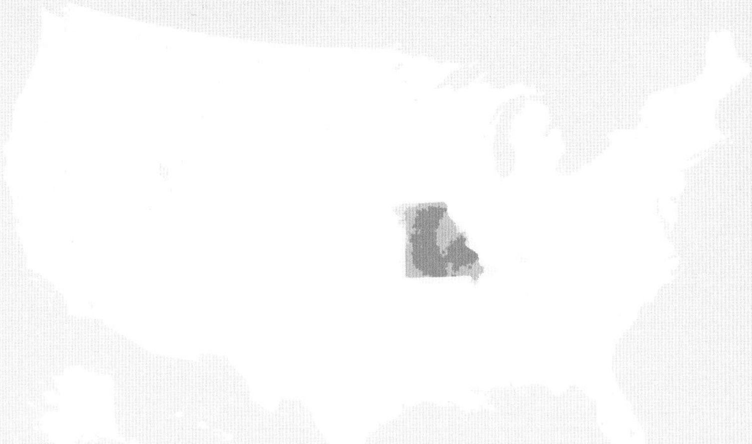

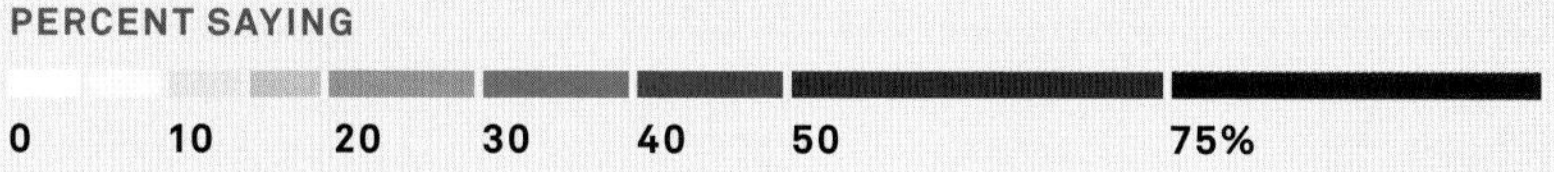

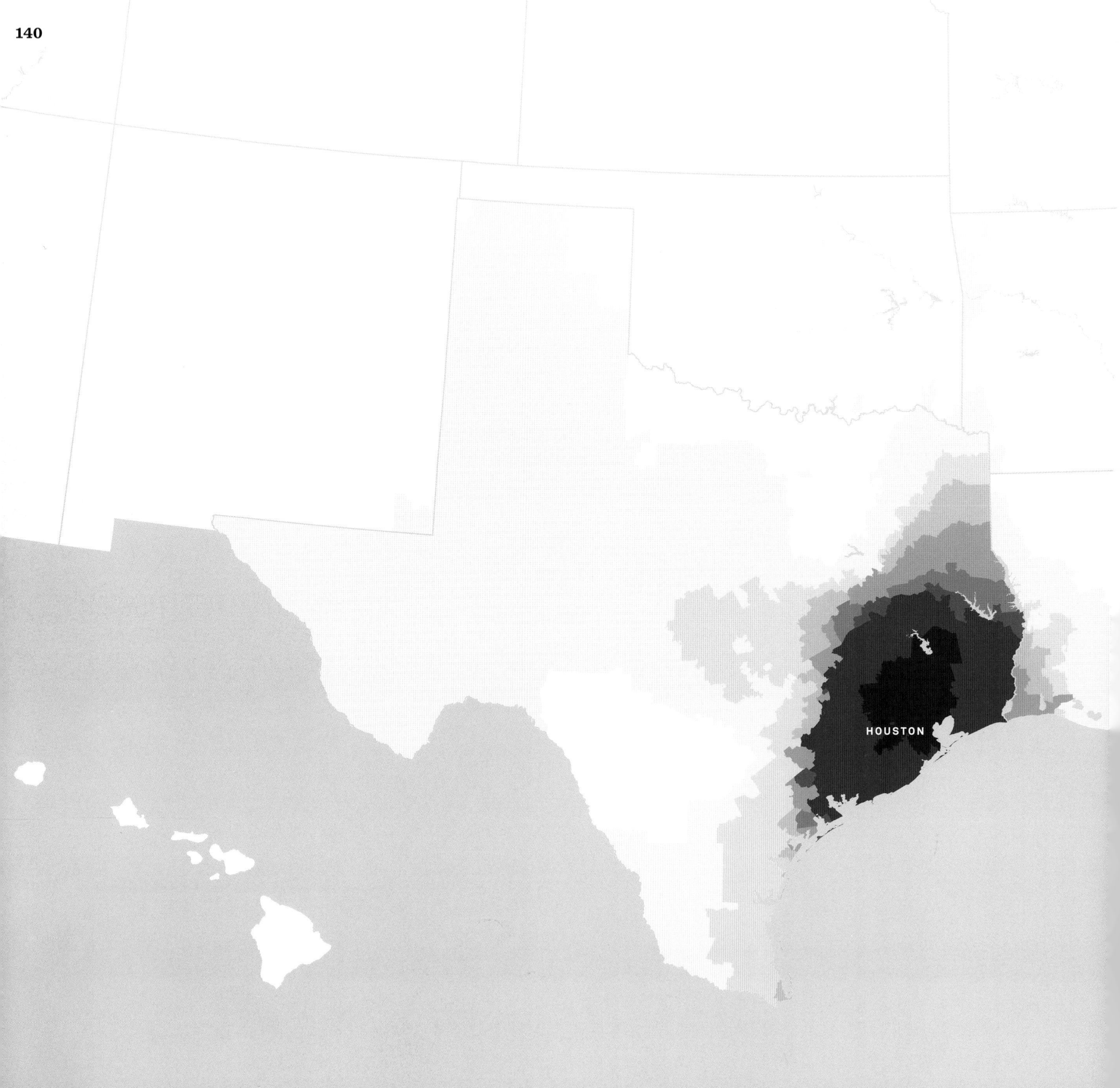
HOUSTON

FEEDER ROAD

While as little as 3 percent of the country is likely to use the term *feeder road*, this term dominates in and around **HOUSTON**. More than 80 percent of the population would choose it.

PERCENT SAYING *FEEDER ROAD*

0 10 20 30 40 50 75%

HOW WE DRIVE IN CIRCLES

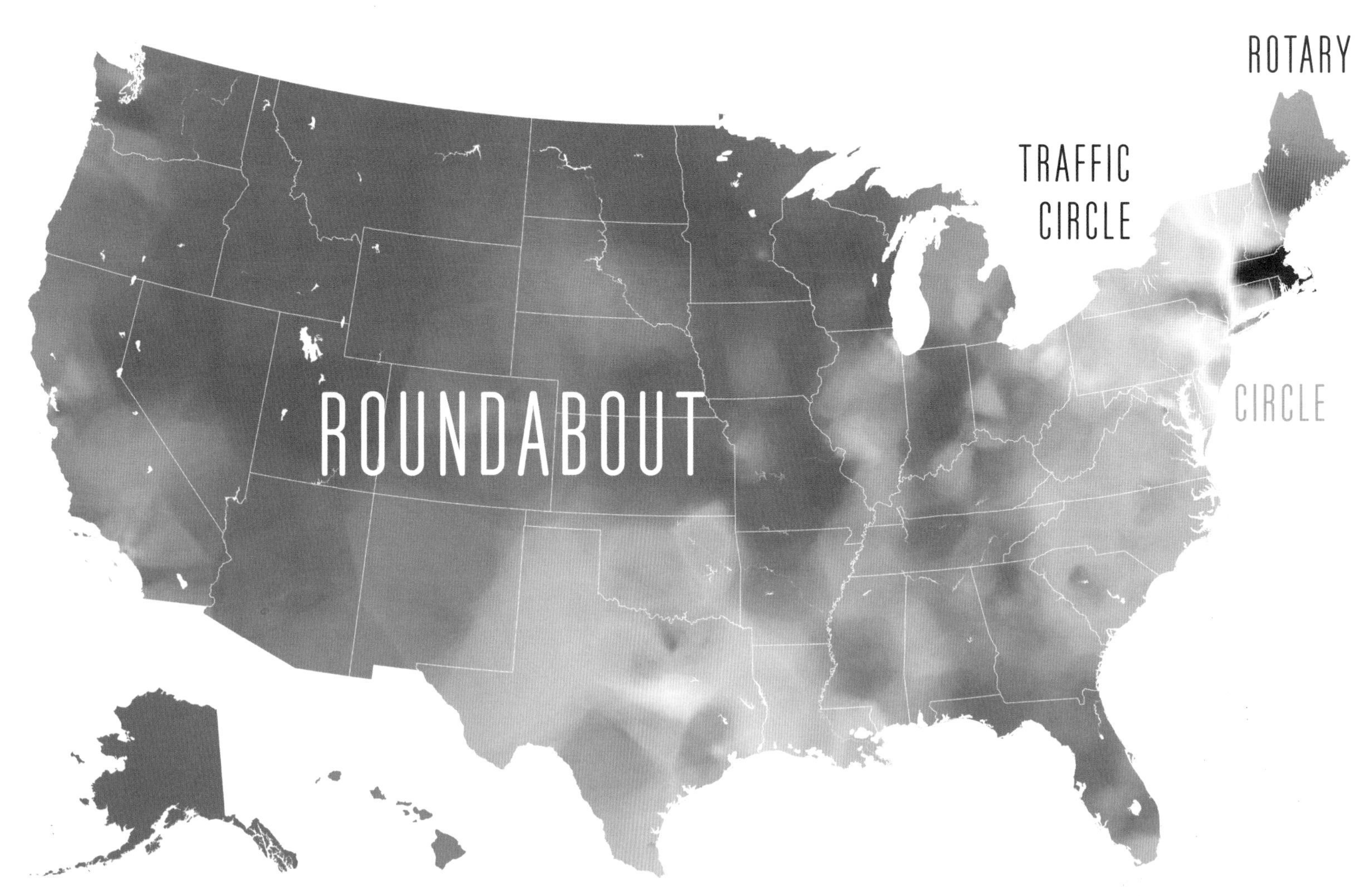

The use of *roundabout* has spread throughout the country over the course of the past century.

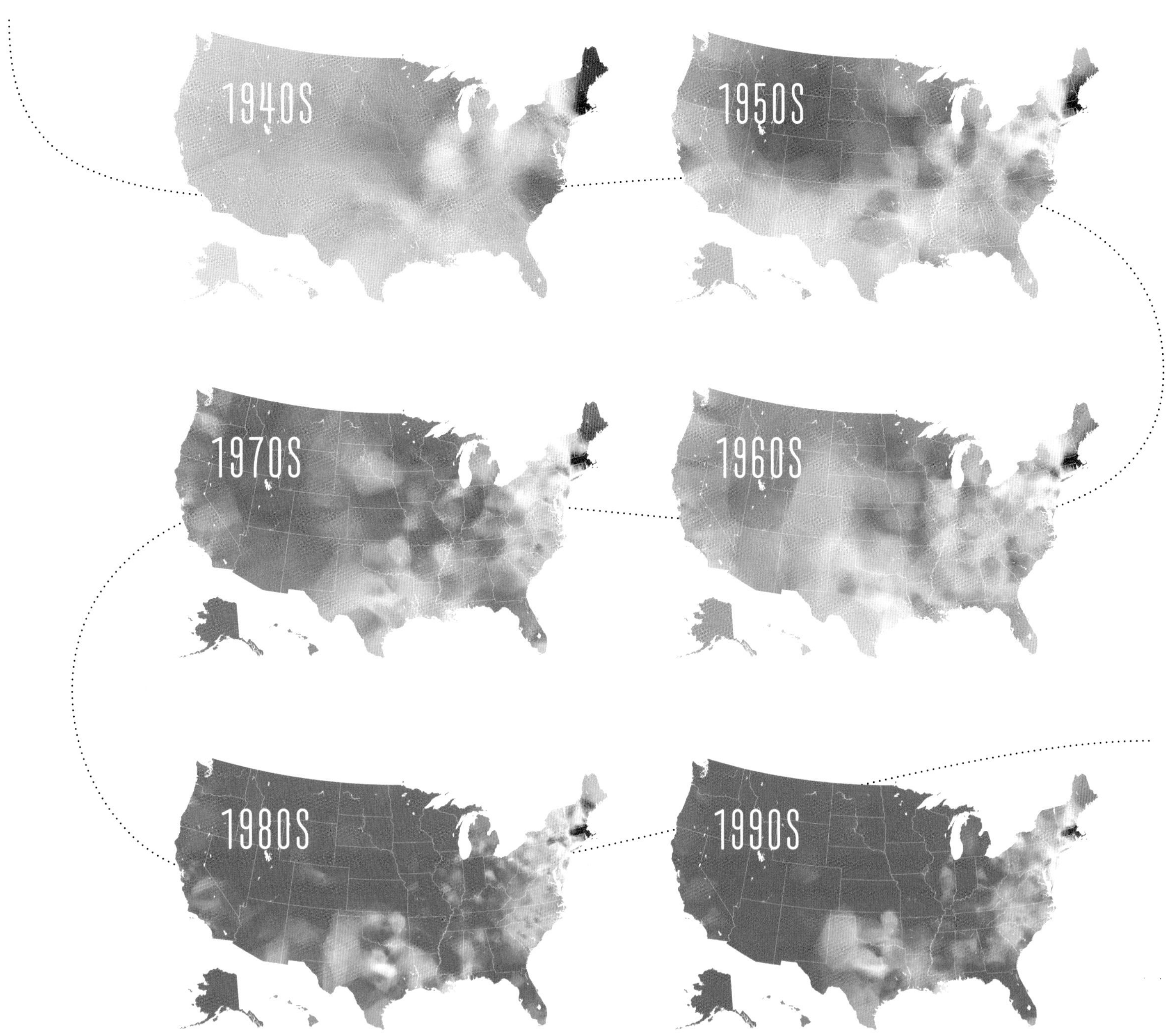

ROUNDABOUT 55%

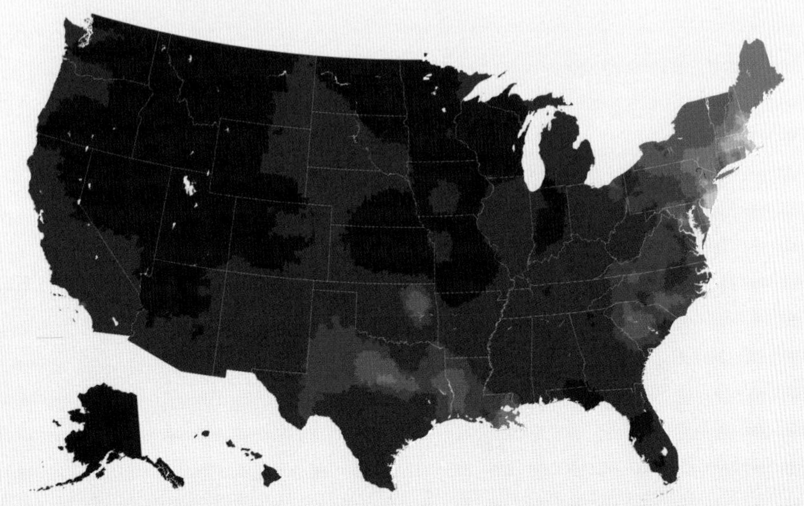

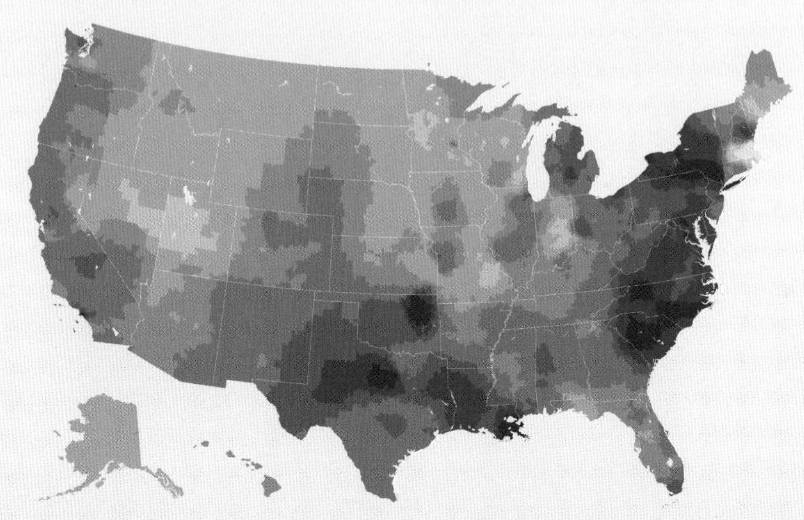

ROTARY 7%

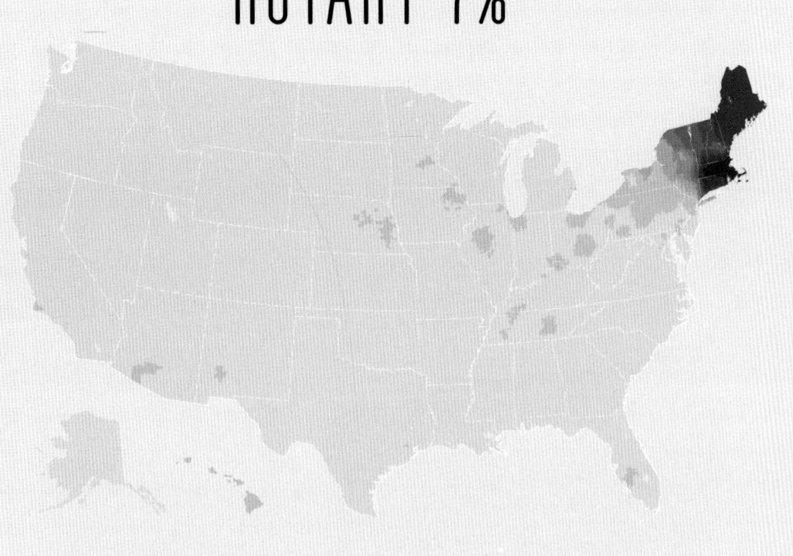

CIRCLE 5%

Some of the final holdouts against *roundabout* are in the **NORTHEAST**. **MASSACHUSETTS** and **MAINE** have their *rotaries,* and **NEW YORK**, eastern **NEW HAMPSHIRE**, and elsewhere have their *traffic circles*. In **SOUTH JERSEY**, on the other hand, the word *traffic* is implied, and it's simply called a *circle*.

WHAT WE CALL

THE STRIP OF GRASS BETWEEN THE SIDE-WALK AND THE ROAD

Perhaps no term is as regionally distinct as Clevelanders' word for the strip of grass between the sidewalk and the road.

Almost three-quarters of the country has no word for it at all. But in Cleveland and to some extent in nearby cities like Akron, Ohio, and Erie, Pennsylvania, it's the *tree lawn*.

Other terms for this little grassy bit are scattered around—*berm, parking, verge, devil's strip, terrace*. For my part, I've always called it the *country strip.* But Cleveland is the only place where a majority has a word for the thing at all.

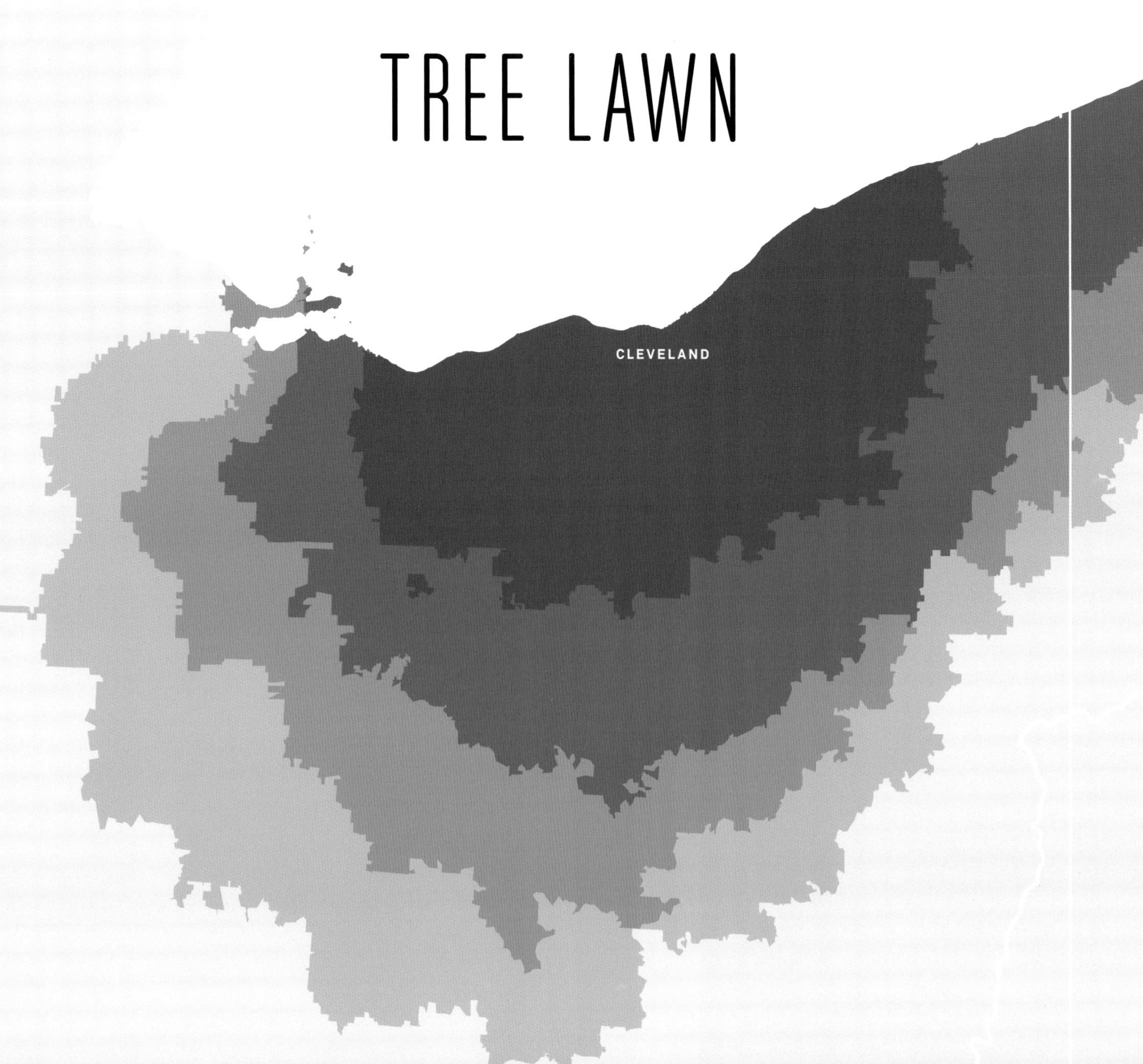
PERCENT SAYING *TREE LAWN*
0
10
20
30
40
>50%
TREE LAWN
CLEVELAND

Perhaps people only acquire this knowledge in their later years or perhaps the term is on the decline, but the younger you are, the less likely you are to have a word for the strip of grass that those from Cleveland usually call the *tree lawn*.

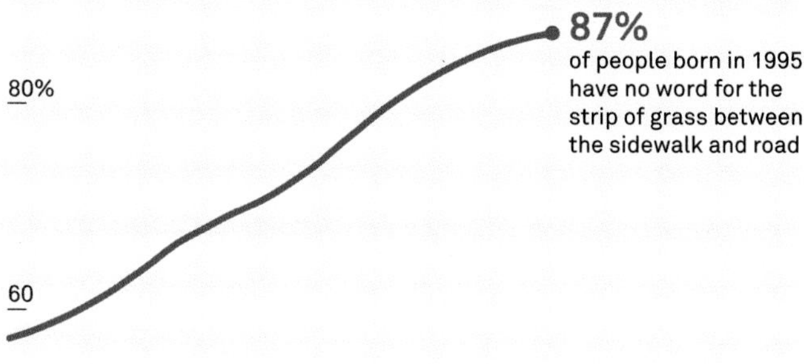

WHAT WE CALL THAT STRIP OF GRASS IN THE MIDDLE OF THE ROAD

Historians say that the history of *neutral ground* goes all the way back to 1803 and the Louisiana Purchase. At that time, a massive influx of English-speaking migrants descended on New Orleans, joining the French and Spanish inhabitants of the city. The newcomers settled upriver, on the other side of a long strip of land intended to become a canal.

Real tension existed between the two groups—fights were common, intermarriage was not. But envoys from the French and Spanish sections of New Orleans would meet at this *neutral ground* to conduct business. The canal was never built, and the land instead became Canal Street, a major thoroughfare with a median.

But the name *neutral ground* stuck, and it continues to this day to serve as the term for a grass strip running down the middle of a road. While widespread in New Orleans itself, with more than 90 percent of people using the phrase, the use of *neutral ground* fades sharply as you leave the city limits. Even in Baton Rouge, only 80 miles away, the share of those using *neutral ground* is only 45 percent.

PERCENT SAYING

0 10 20 30 40 50 75%

BOULEVARD

WHAT WE CALL

A DRIVE-THROUGH LIQUOR STORE

For years before the first McDonald's drive-thru opened in 1975, Americans had been buying liquor from their cars at drive-through liquor stores. They're unknown in much of the country but go by a variety of names in Texas and pockets of the Deep South.

If you're looking to buy beer without leaving the comfort of your vehicle, in and around Dallas, throughout Mississippi, and in Tallahassee, you'd head to a *beer barn*.

But in the expanse of country west of San Antonio, you'd head to a *beverage barn* instead, as you would in Tampa, Florida.

Though if you're going to come up with a name for a drive-through liquor store, *party barn* is pretty good. So well done, Corpus Christi.

NO WORD FOR THIS 77%

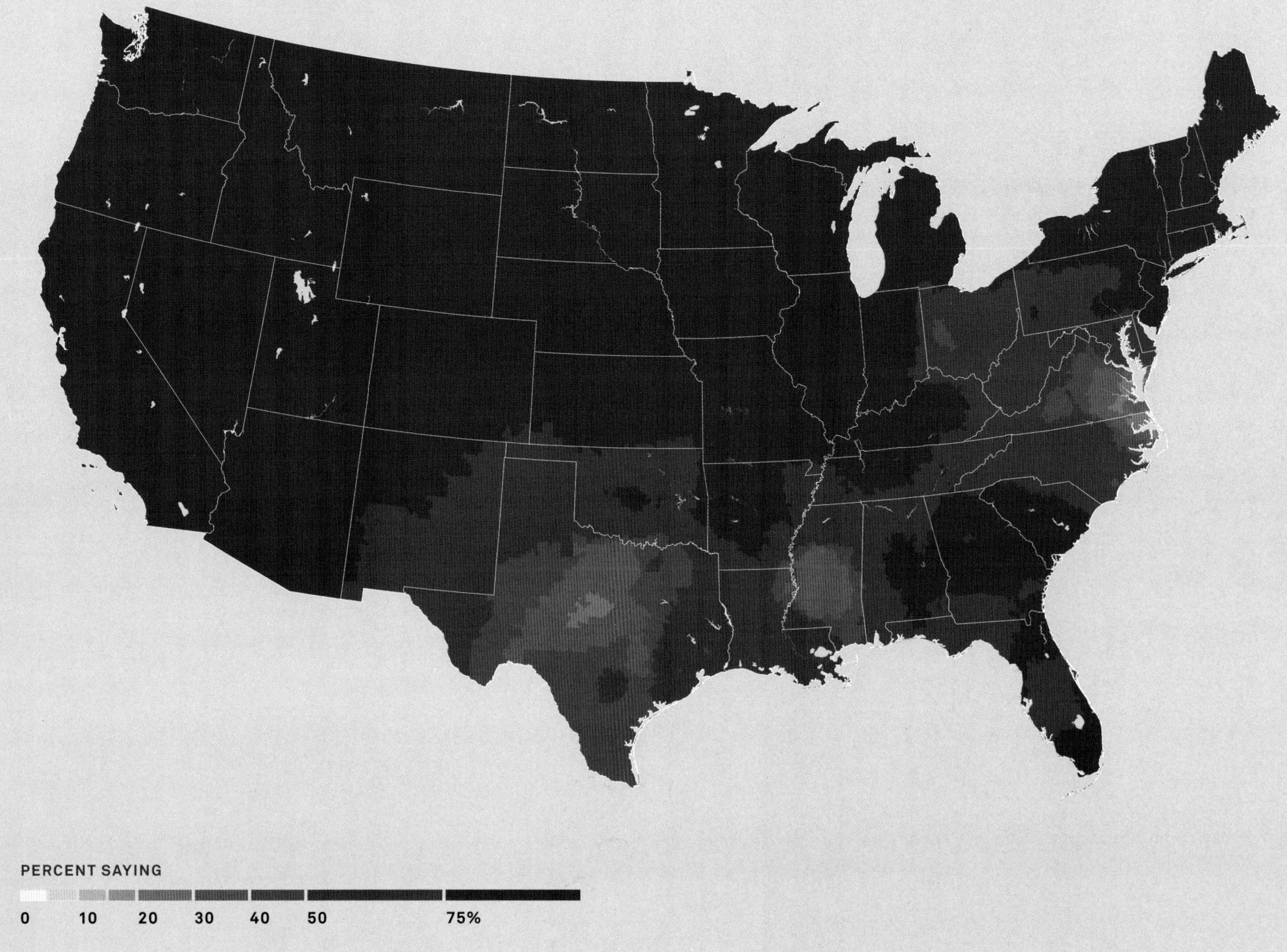

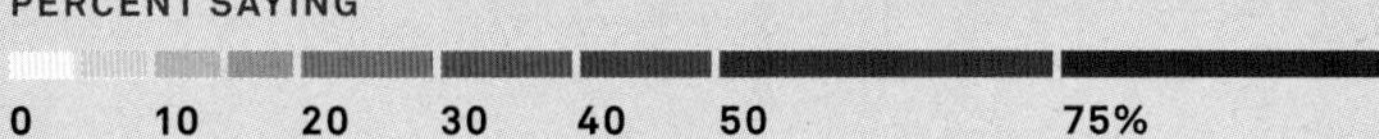

BEER BARN 6%

BREW THRU 6%

PARTY BARN 1%

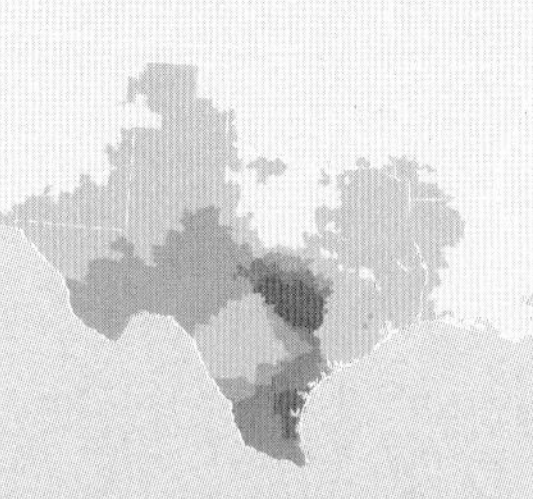

BEVERAGE BARN 1%

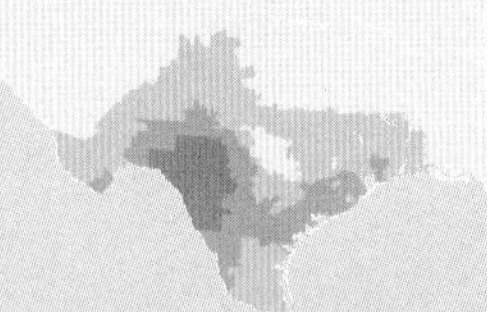

TRANSIT NETWORK TRICKERY

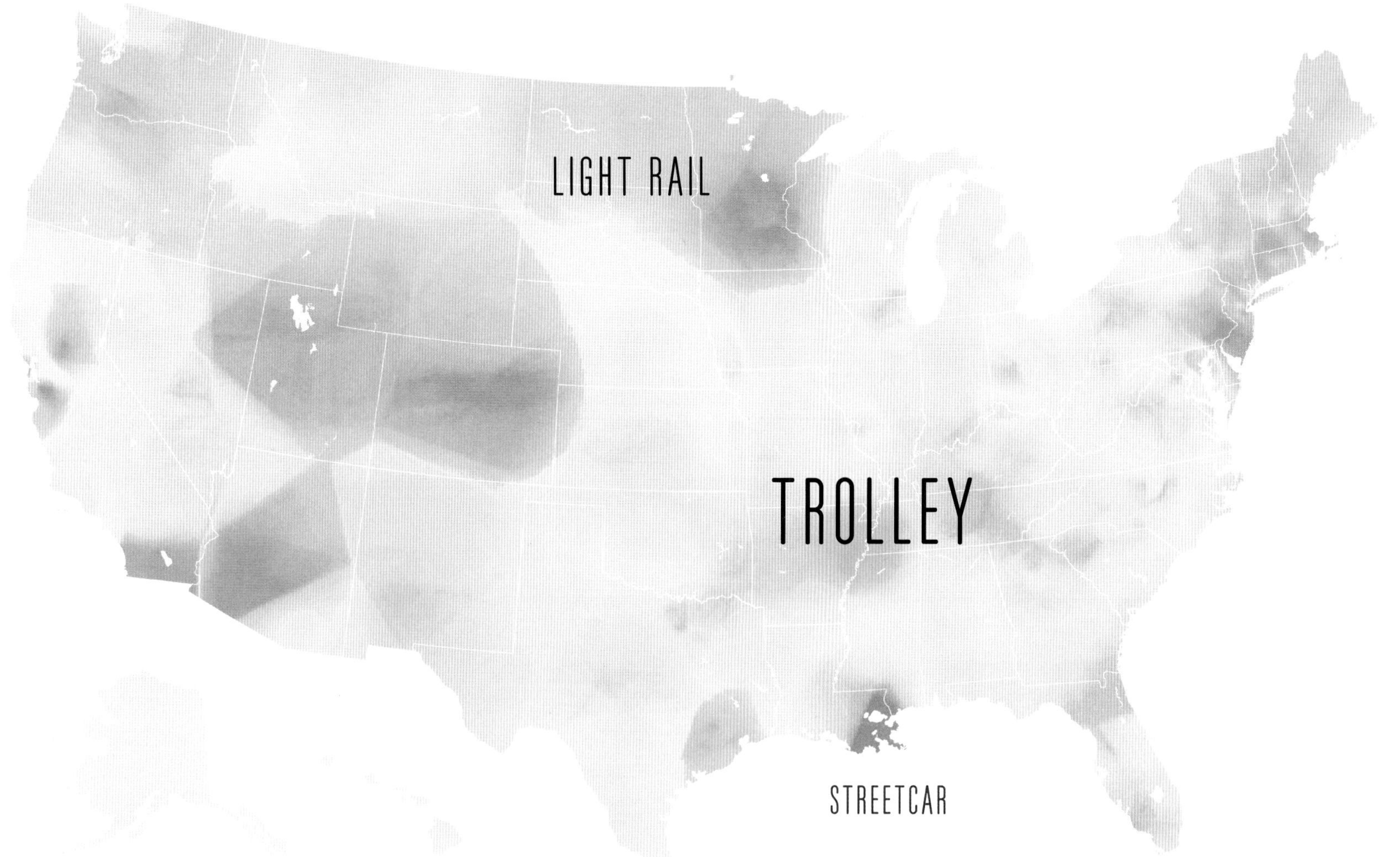
LIGHT RAIL
TROLLEY
STREETCAR

METRO 3%

NO WORD FOR THIS 3%

TRAM 9%

LIGHT RAIL 12%

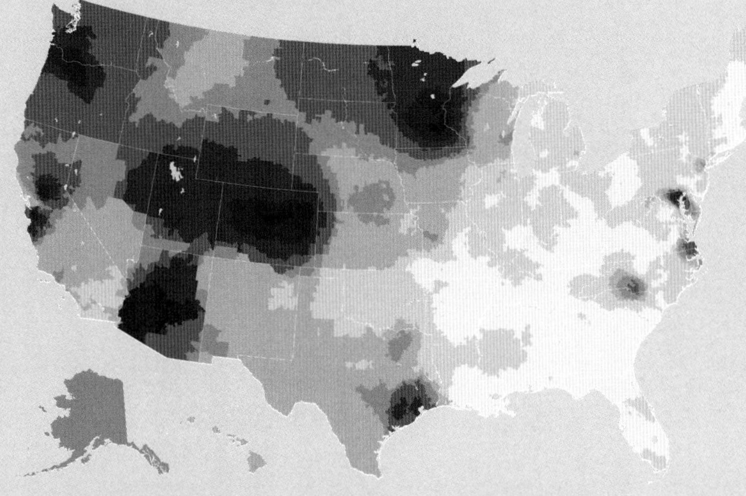

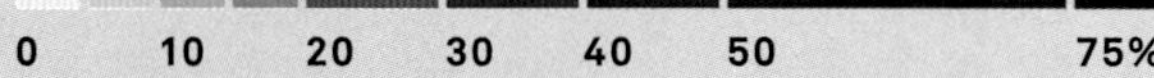

CABLE CAR 4%

TRAIN 6%

TROLLEY 34%

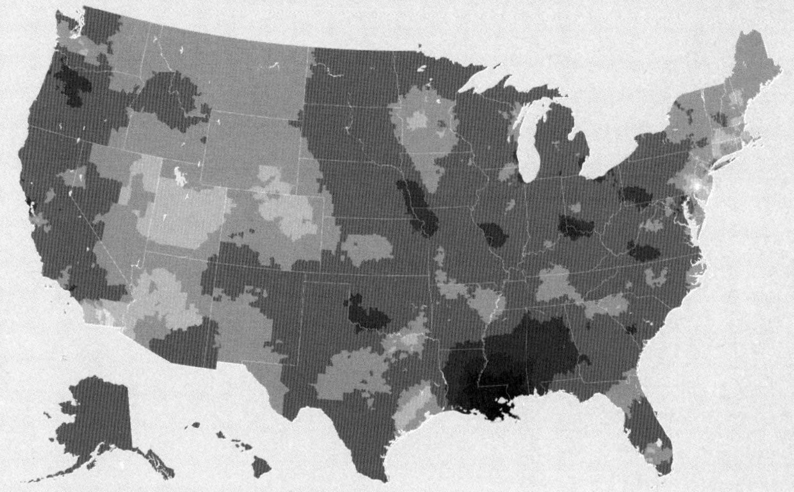

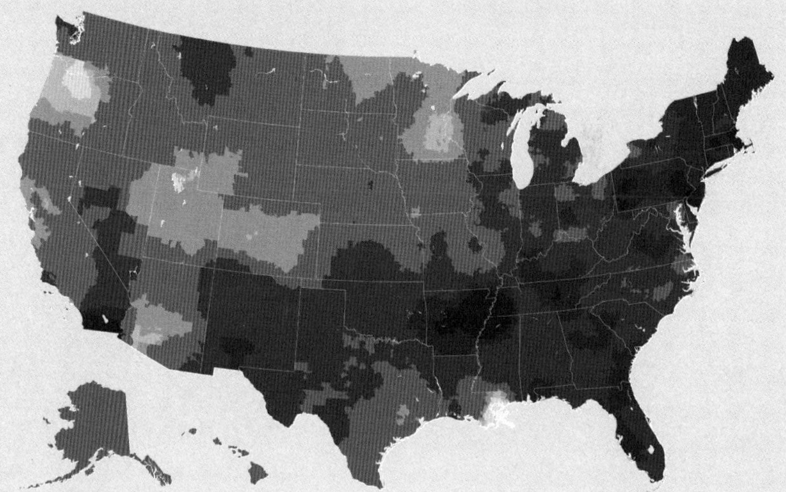

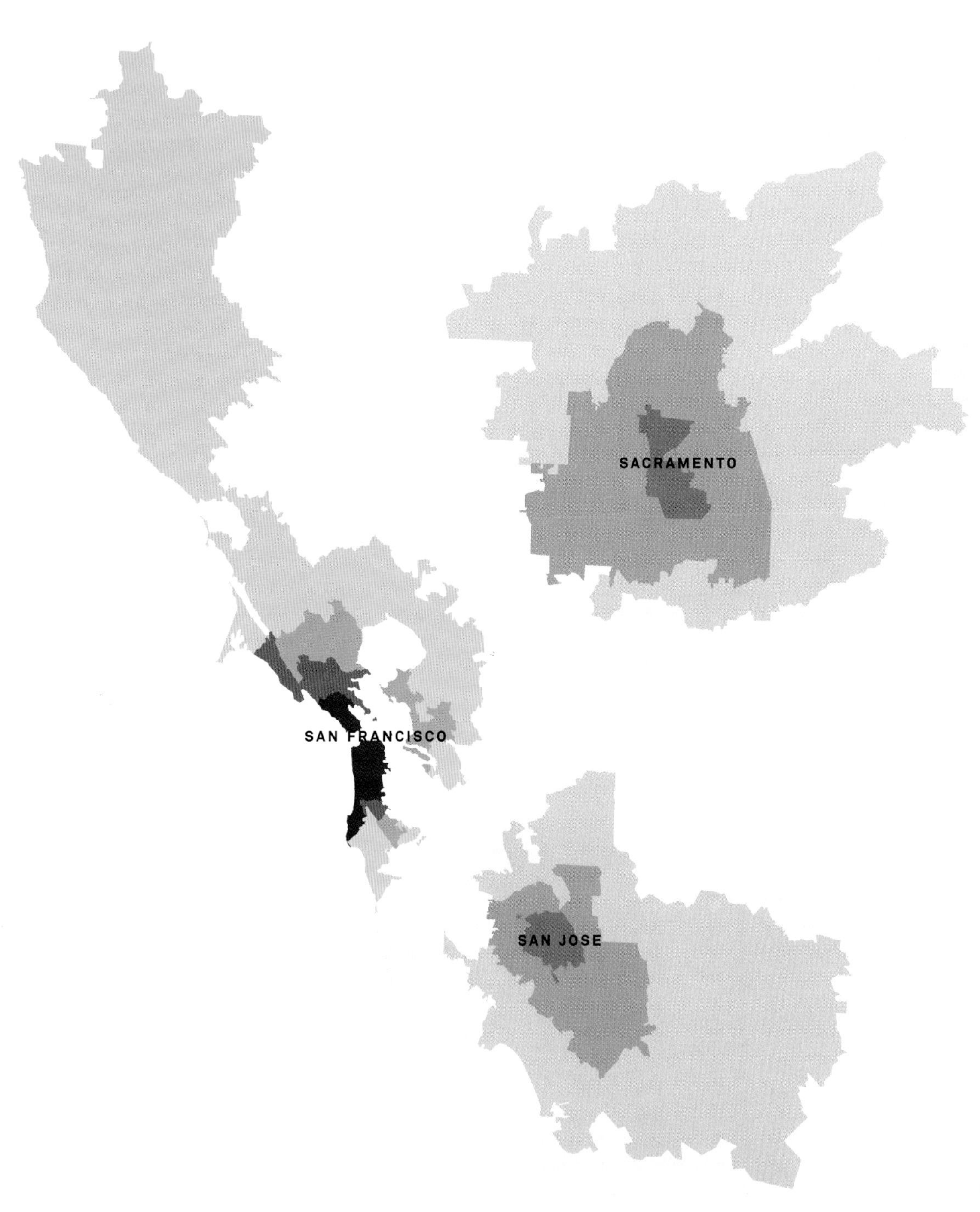
SACRAMENTO
SAN FRANCISCO
SAN JOSE

A STREETCAR NAMED *LIGHT RAIL*

In 1888, Frank J. Sprague's streetcar design, which used a trolley wheel, or *troller,* to feed electricity from overhead wires to the streetcar engine, revolutionized urban travel. Within a year, Sprague's *trolley car* was in place in more than 150 railway systems in the United States. The change ushered in the modern American city. People no longer had to live within a short distance of their jobs. Suddenly, communities began to spring up 15 or 20 miles from the center of the city.

The rise of the automobile in the 1940s and '50s sent many streetcars into retirement, and almost all of the original lines closed. But in recent years the light rail has undergone something of a renaissance, with many cities building new rail lines. It has become popular again as urban living has become more popular.

What people call the light rail car is often a product of the name of their city's light rail network. San Diego has *trolleys* (from the San Diego Trolley, the first of the second wave of light rail lines, which began service in 1981). Sacramento and San Jose have *light rails.* San Francisco, less than 100 miles away, has *streetcars.*

These terms also vary across the country, with little geographic cohesion. Philadelphia and Memphis have *trolleys*. On Team Light Rail: Denver, Minneapolis, and Phoenix. On Team Streetcar: New Orleans and Cincinnati. And with the Portland Streetcar system joining the city's MAX Light Rail in 2001, that city now shows an almost even split.

Some rail enthusiasts argue that there are semantic distinctions among the terms, with *light rail* denoting a faster, higher-capacity service with longer distances between stations. But that notion doesn't always match reality. San Diego's *trolleys,* to take just one example, move as fast as Sacramento's *light rail,* with stations spread farther apart.

WHERE WE SHOP

GROH-SERY STORE

GROH-SHERY STORE

GROH-SERY STORE

In and around Boston, New York, and Philadelphia, you're more likely to hear *groh-sery store.* But in much of the country, the (once non-standard) *groh-shery store* pronunciation dominates. What's more, the pronunciation with the *sh* sound is on the rise: nearly two-thirds of Americans born in 1995 or later use it, suggesting the alternate pronunciation could one day become the norm.

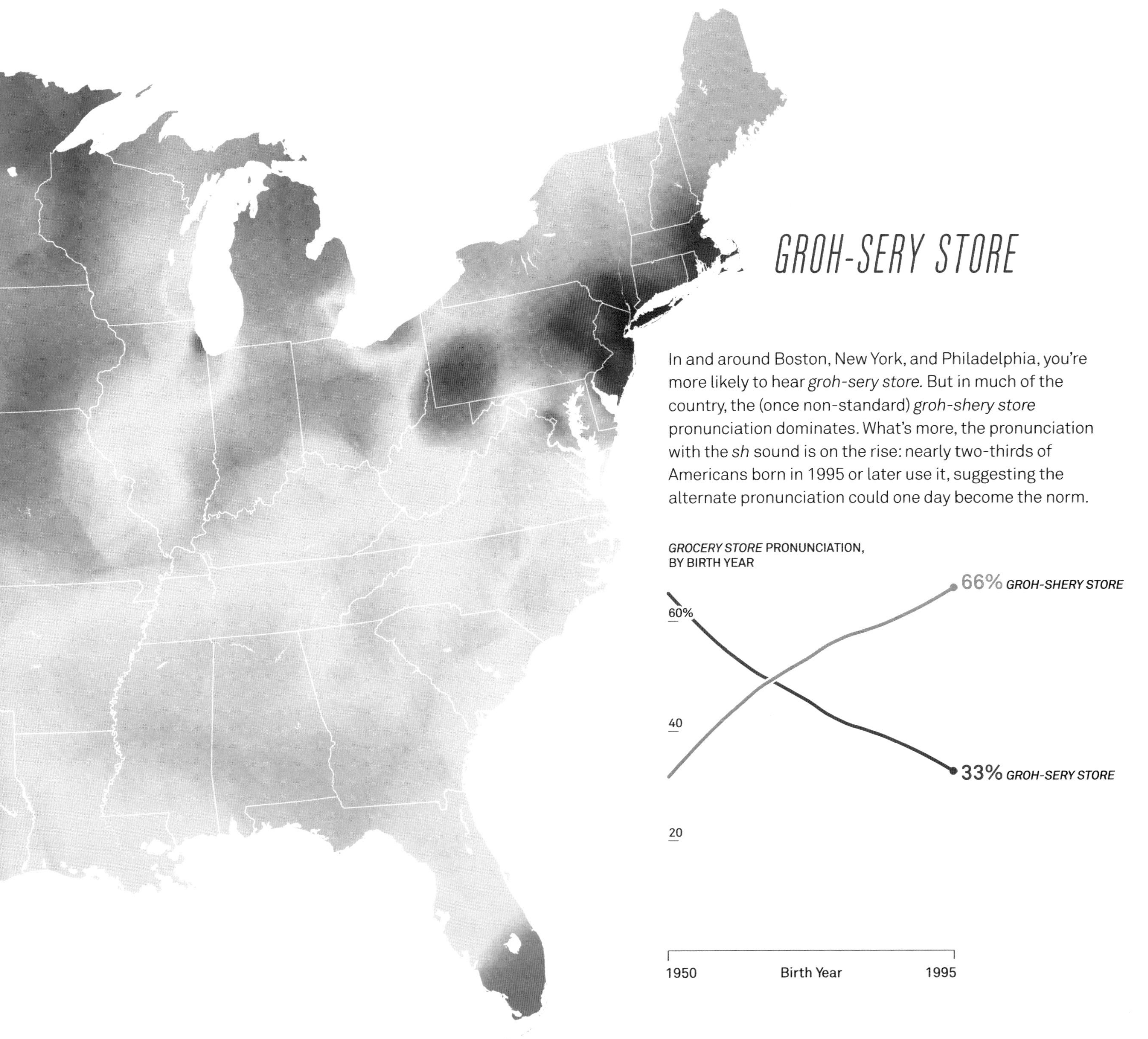

WHAT WE PUT OUR STUFF IN WHILE WE SHOP

In 1937, Sylvan Goldman devised a way that customers at his Humpty Dumpty supermarket in Oklahoma City could hold more groceries. What you might call a *carriage* in Massachusetts or a *grocery cart* in Nebraska is most commonly known as a *shopping cart*. In Alabama, however, more than 40 percent of people call it a *buggy*.

Goldman's cart wasn't an immediate success. It reminded many women of a baby carriage, and some men felt it insulted their masculinity, writes Ellen Ruppel Shell in her book *Cheap: The High Cost of Discount Culture*. Others feared that the soiled diapers of babies sitting in the front of the carts would make the carts unsanitary. Goldman persisted, however, handing people the carts as they entered and even hiring people to push loaded carts back and forth in front of his store as a demonstration. Eventually, the cart became a staple of the American retail experience, making Goldman a millionaire in the process.

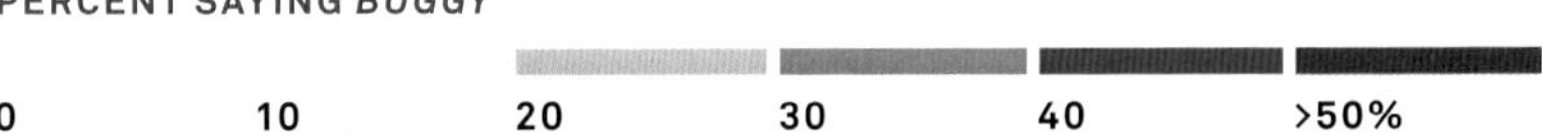
PERCENT SAYING *BUGGY*
0
10
20
30
40
>50%

HOW TO PRETEND YOU'RE FROM

LOUISIANA

The distinct cultures and influences of New Orleans—French, Spanish, creole—blend together to make English sound different here than it does pretty much anywhere else in the country. The influence of French—more specifically, Cajun French—is everywhere. In some parishes, more than a quarter of the population speaks French at home.

Many of their dialect words come from their local foods: *gumbo* and *jambalaya,* and *po'boys* and *beignets,* of course, as well as *daube glace* (a chilled, jellied beef or veal stew, usually served as an appetizer with sliced French bread).

The distinct patois of New Orleans is not all about food, though. There's also *neutral ground, crawfish* (not *crawdads* or *crayfish*), and *doodlebugs*. Louisiana doesn't have *Mischief Night,* but if it did, you might go *rolling* (covering houses in toilet paper). The state is the one place where people refer to the end of a loaf of bread as the *nose* and where *aunt* might sound like *ain't*.

A *lagniappe* (pronounced *lan-yap*) is a small gift that often accomanies a purchase. It's a word with definitive creole origins: From the indigenous Quechua language of South America, Spanish colonizers got *la ñapa* (meaning extra or bonus). After several centuries of mixing with French, *la ñapa* transmogrified into *lagniappe*. It is, as Mark Twain wrote in *Life on the Mississippi,* "one excellent word—a word worth traveling to New Orleans to get."

HOW TO PRETEND YOU'RE FROM

THE DEEP SOUTH

Dialect-wise, the deepest part of the Deep South comprises Alabama, Mississippi, western Tennessee, and the eastern half of Arkansas.

Around here, you might toss some *cocola* (soda) into your *buggy* (shopping cart) and then stop off for some *flap-jacks* (pancakes). Less than 2 percent of people in the Deep South still use the word *flapjacks,* but of all those in America who say *flapjacks* instead of *pancakes,* almost a quarter of them are from around here. Residents of the region are also fond of *Lane cake,* a buttery layer cake with white frosting and a large helping of bourbon.

You might be from the Deep South if you:

- call covering someone's house in toilet paper *rolling,*
- say *eighteen-wheeler,* and
- use one of the more colorful expressions for when it rains while the sun is shining, like *monkey's wedding, the wolf giving birth,* or *the devil beating his wife.*

HOW TO PRETEND YOU'RE FROM

GEORGIA

Georgia speech can be tough to distinguish from the words alone, particularly because the dialect of Atlanta is so different from that of the surrounding countryside. In many respects, speech in Atlanta bears more resemblance to that of Raleigh, North Carolina. Both cities show more of a northern tilt, thanks in large part to the influx of notherners over the years.

Of course, Georgia has its own particular food terms: *chicken mull* (a creamy chicken stew, various versions of which can be found scattered around Georgia and North Carolina) and *egg bread* (cornbread made with eggs) among them. And don't forget *crip course* (an easy class), *access road,* and *buggy* (shopping cart); if you hear those three together, there's a 50 percent chance you're talking to someone from Georgia.

HOW TO PRETEND YOU'RE FROM

SOUTH CAROLINA

Charleston, South Carolina, was a major city in colonial times—one of the original six linguistic centers of the United States.

South Carolina is also home to the endangered language of Gullah, which can still be heard out in the Lowcountry and Sea Islands of South Carolina and Georgia. It developed among West African slaves working the coastal plantations, a combination of English and West African languages like Fula and Mende that became a distinct creole. The islands' geographic isolation allowed the community to develop a way of speaking distinct enough from everyday American English to become its own language. While the population of Gullah speakers numbers around 250,000, most do not speak it as their first language. The most recent census puts the number of people speaking Gullah at home at fewer than one thousand. About one-third of all Gullah speakers live in South Carolina, and the other two-thirds live in New York.

HOW TO PRETEND YOU'RE FROM

NORTH CAROLINA

There are not *garage sales* here, only *yard sales.* People don't say *semi* or *frontage road*. It's distinctly *y'all* territory, and it remains one of the places you're most likely to hear someone say they *might could* do something (a construction known as a *double modal*).

As is the case with Georgia, North Carolina is linguistically divided between a more northern-influenced urban area (the Research Triangle) and a surrounding countryside. There's the Outer Banks, the middle section around Raleigh and Chapel Hill (the Research Triangle), and in the western portion of the state, which more closely resembles eastern Tennessee than central North Carolina, you'll find that the dialect has an Appalachian tinge. As you move east, toward the Outer Banks, you're more likely to find someone familiar with the local *brew thru*.

Just to the southeast of the Research Triangle is where you're most likely to hear someone call an easy class a *crip course*. In addition, if you hear someone say *tractor-trailer* and use *granddaddy* for the long-legged spidery-looking thing that I'd call a *daddy longlegs,* there's a 50-50 chance you're talking to someone from North Carolina.

HOW TO PRETEND YOU'RE FROM

FLORIDA

Florida is really more like two linguistic states, with the dividing line between north and south running from Port St. Lucie on the Atlantic coast roughly southwest through Lake Okeechobee (a name derived from the Hitchiti words for *big* and *water*) to Fort Myers and the Gulf of Mexico. An old cliché about Florida holds that "the farther north you go, the farther south you get," and it applies to speech too. The northern region speaks something closer to a southern dialect while the southern region speaks something closer to a northern dialect. Southern Florida is also notable for the influence of Spanish immigrants. Over 90 percent of people in Hialeah, just west of Miami, speak Spanish in the home.

Florida's speech divide follows the more subtle aspects of the entire country's northern and southern dialects. Of the Floridians who use the word *supper,* call the bug that curls up into a little ball when touched a *roly-poly,* and don't use the word *sunshower,* 80 percent of them are from northern rather than southern Florida.

But enough coherence still exists between the two halves of the state to give Floridian speech its own character. The biggest unifier is *panther.* Half of those who say *panther* instead of *mountain lion* are from Florida, as are 75 percent of those who, in addition to saying *panther,* use *scallion* over *green onion* (usually restricted more to the northeastern states) and know about drive-through liquor stores but don't have a special word for them.

5

Part Five

THINGS WE SEE

WHAT WE CALL

THE INSECTS THAT GLOW AT NIGHT

Judging people by their speech is nothing new. In the 1800s, British writers scorned their American counterparts for their peculiar habits, such as calling a wide variety of different insects *bugs:* thus we had May bugs, June bugs, and, of course, *lightning bugs*.

The term *lightning bug,* well known in America since at least 1778, was never universally adopted in the country, and even today its use offers one of the few examples of a sharp divide among the boroughs of New York City. Manhattanites tend to eschew the Americanism in favor of the more British *firefly,* while the denizens of Staten Island take their cue from New Jersey and stick with *lightning bug*.

Yet some evidence suggests that *lightning bug*'s days may be numbered: Though it is twice as popular as *firefly* among speakers born in the 1950s, for those born in the 1990s the ratio is flipped.

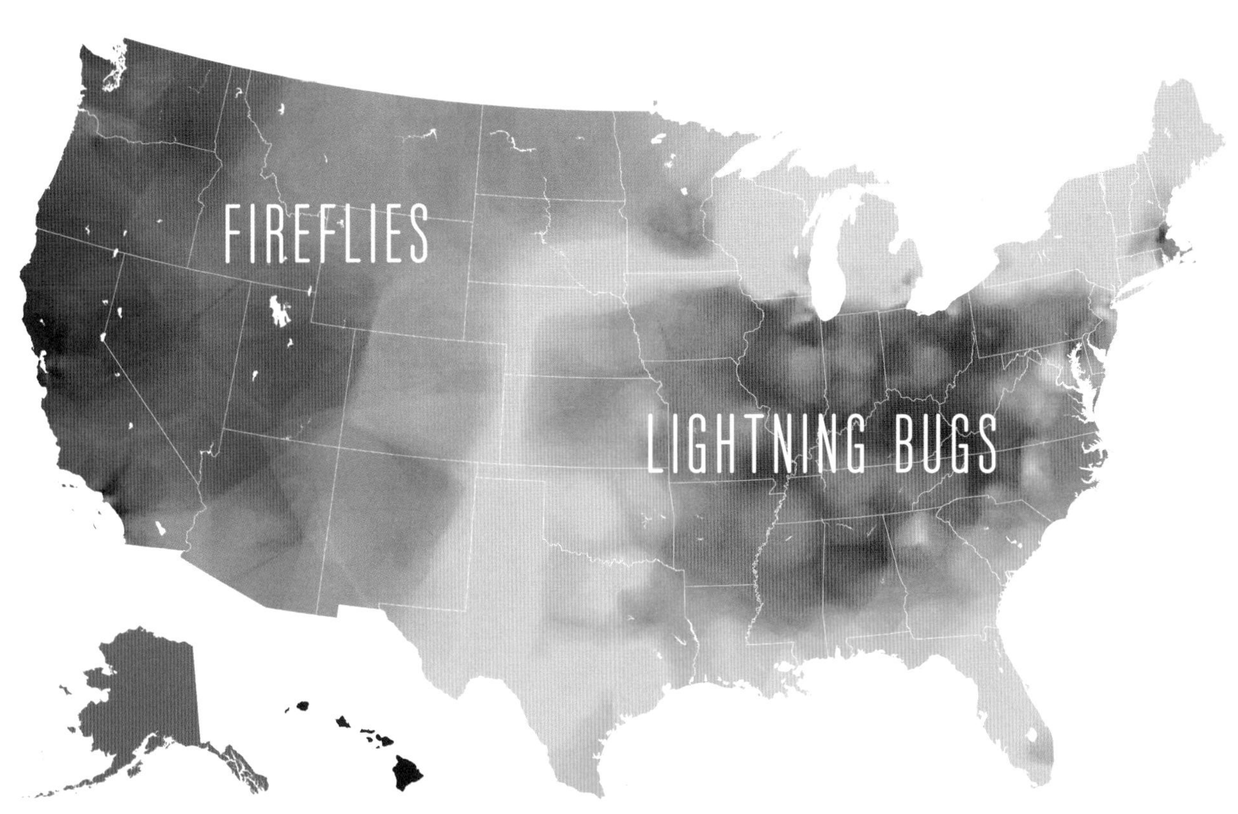

In **MANHATTAN** more people tend to say *firefly*.

In **STATEN ISLAND** and **NEW JERSEY** you're more likely to hear someone say *lightning bug*.

NO MORE LIGHTNING BUGS?

Over the past century, the part of the country where speakers are more likely to say *firefly* has expanded.

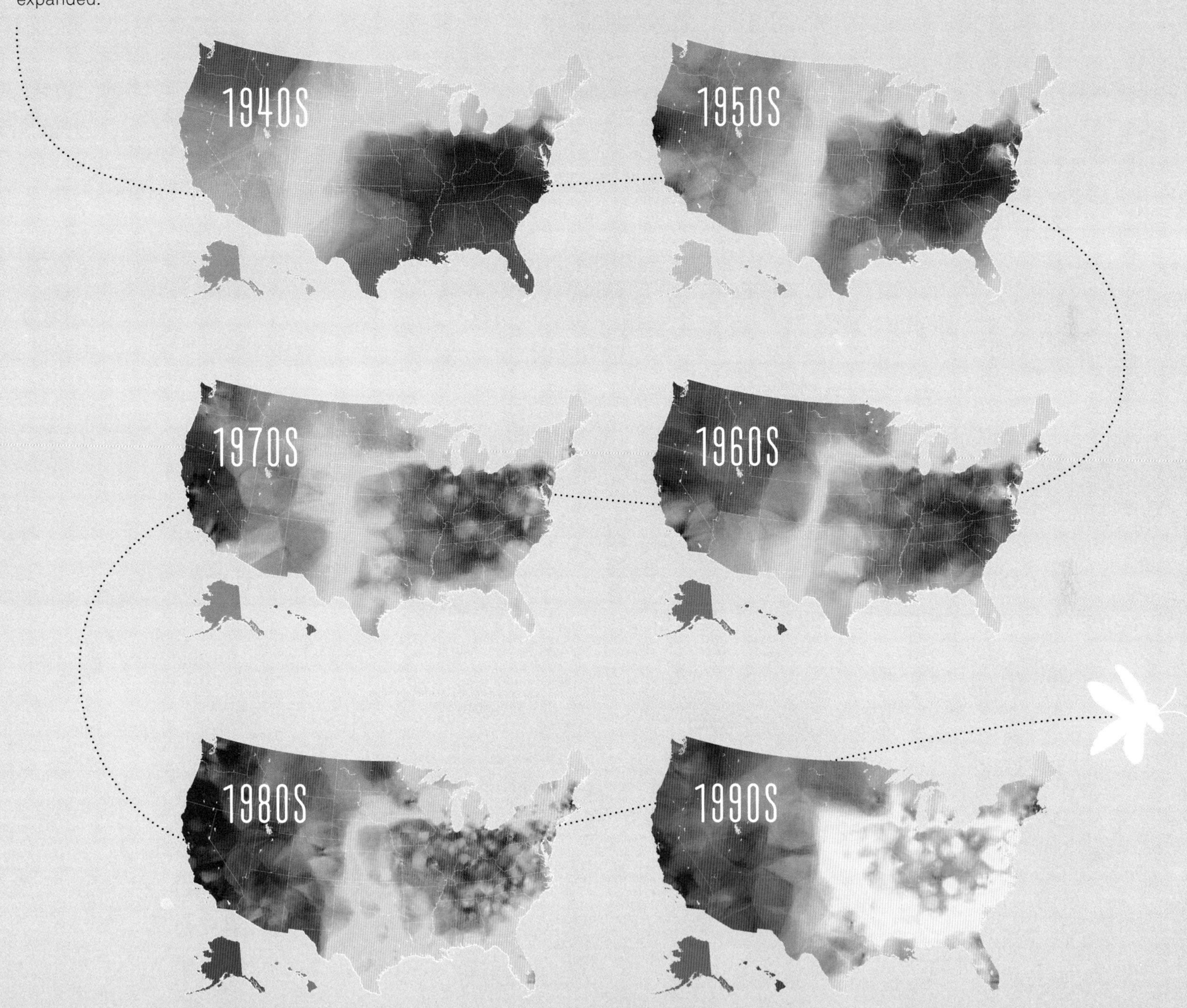

A PHIL BY ANY OTHER NAME WOULD BE AS ACCURATE

Most of the country prefers *groundhog*, particularly the Appalachian region around West Virginia and western Pennsylvania, home to the country's largest Groundhog Day celebration and most famous groundhog: Punxsutawney Phil.

Groundhog Day, celebrated on February 2, derives from the ancient Christian tradition of Candlemas Day. The Pennsylvania Dutch, seventeenth- and eighteenth-century German immigrants who came to Pennsylvania speaking Deutsch, brought the tradition to the United States.

Despite the ubiquity of the holiday, people in New York, New England, and parts of the upper Midwest more often call this animal a *woodchuck*.

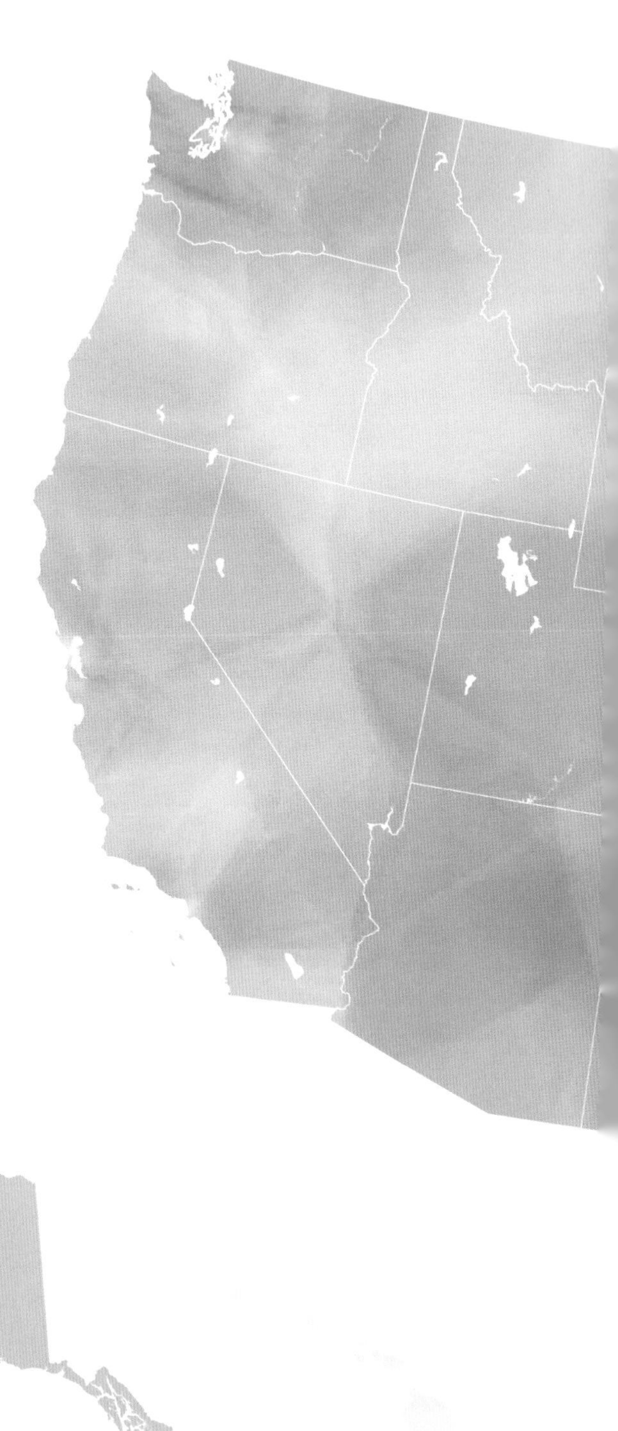

WOODCHUCK
GROUNDHOG

WHAT DO YOU CALL THIS?

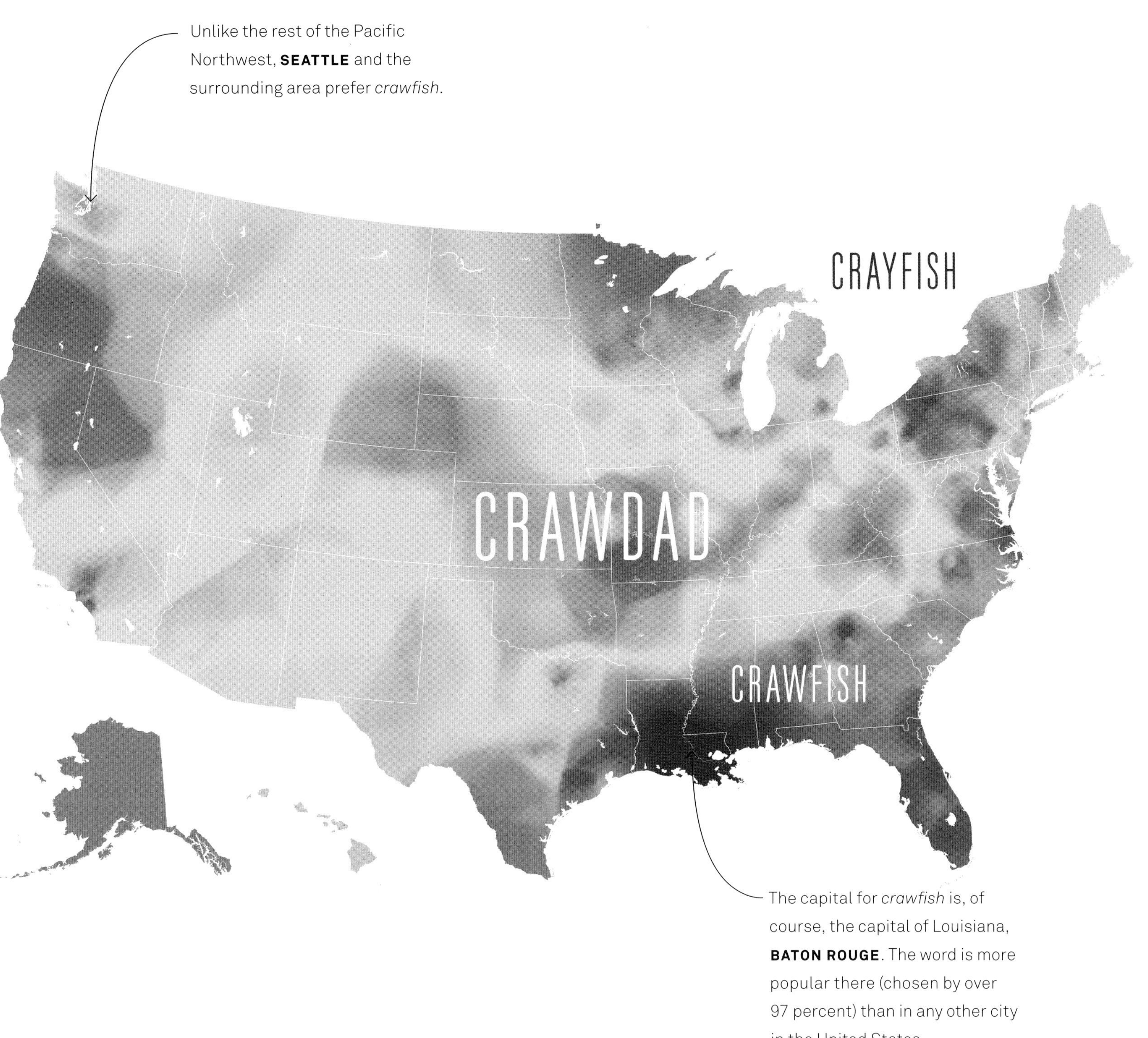
Unlike the rest of the Pacific Northwest, **SEATTLE** and the surrounding area prefer *crawfish*.
CRAYFISH
CRAWDAD
CRAWFISH
The capital for *crawfish* is, of course, the capital of Louisiana, **BATON ROUGE**. The word is more popular there (chosen by over 97 percent) than in any other city in the United States.

CRAWFISH 45%

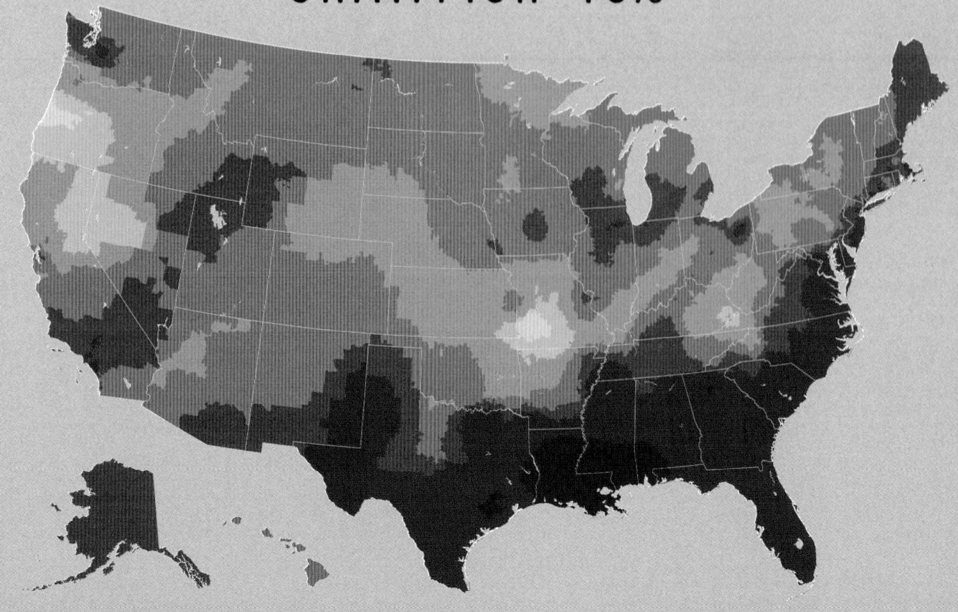

CRAWDAD 28%

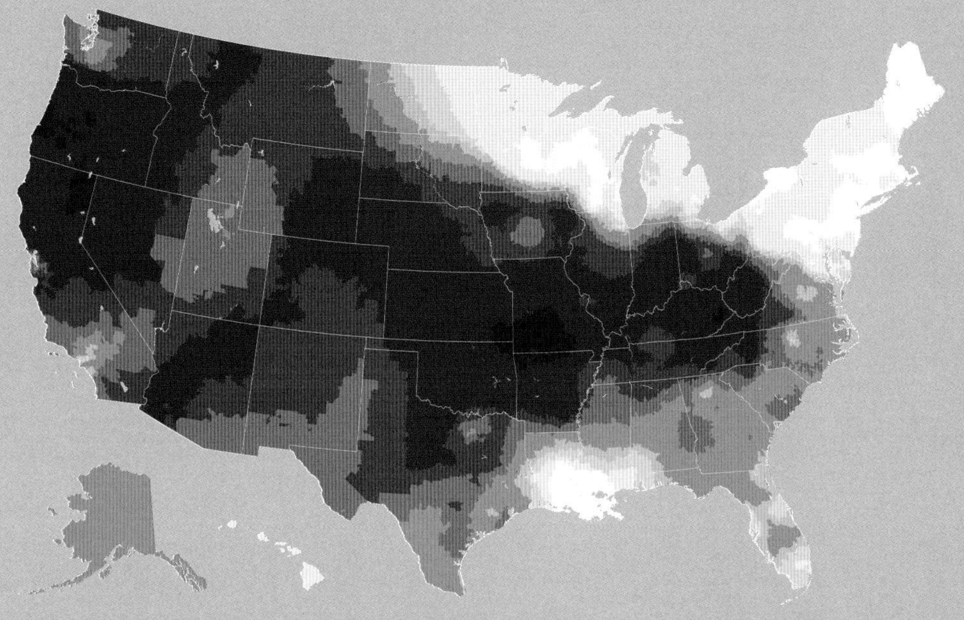

PERCENT SAYING

0 10 20 30 40 50 75%

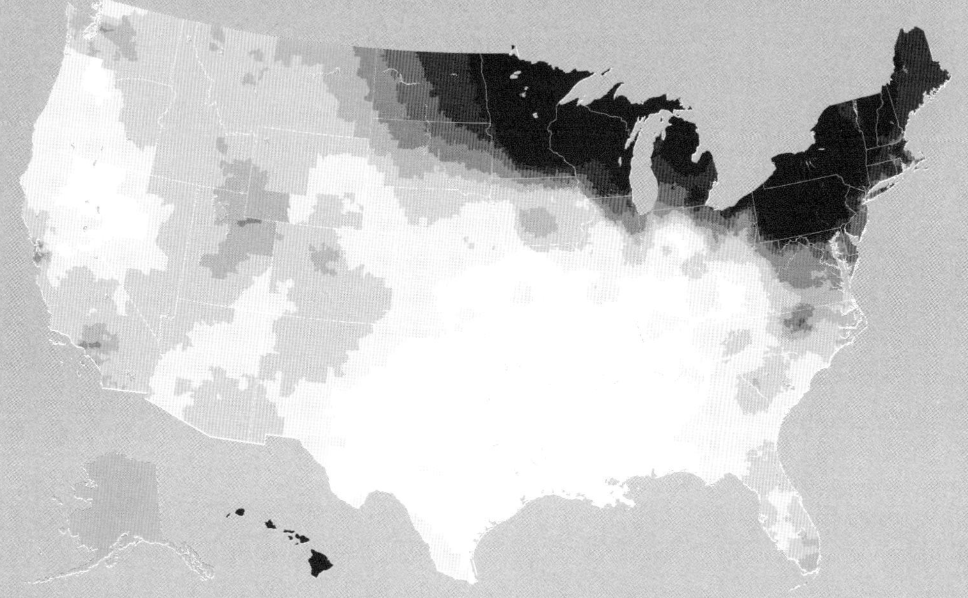

NO WORD FOR THIS 2%

WE DON'T EVEN KNOW

WHAT THIS BUG IS, NEVER MIND WHAT TO CALL IT

The little critter (the woodlouse) isn't technically an insect—surprisingly, it's a crustacean. It is commonly found in the damp, dark spaces underneath rocks and logs, and its most noticeable characteristic is its tendency to curl up into a little ball when disturbed. Hence the name *roly-poly*.

But while *roly-poly* is the most popular name for the bug, er, crustacean, almost half the country prefers another word, with great geographic variation in people's choices. *Pillbug* is the most common response in Cincinnati, and *doodlebug* in New Orleans. In New England, many people have no word for it at all.

And in a seemingly random smattering of places around the country—including western New York, Utah, the Pacific Northwest, and, to a somewhat lesser extent, Pittsburgh, Milwaukee, and Washington, D.C.—you find instead the term *potato bug*. No one I talked to could offer a solid explanation for this odd geographic grouping. For the time being, the mystery of *potato bug* endures.

Once confounding factor to keep in mind: *potato bug* is often applied to at least three different insects—not only the woodlouse but the Jerusalem cricket and the potato beetle as well.

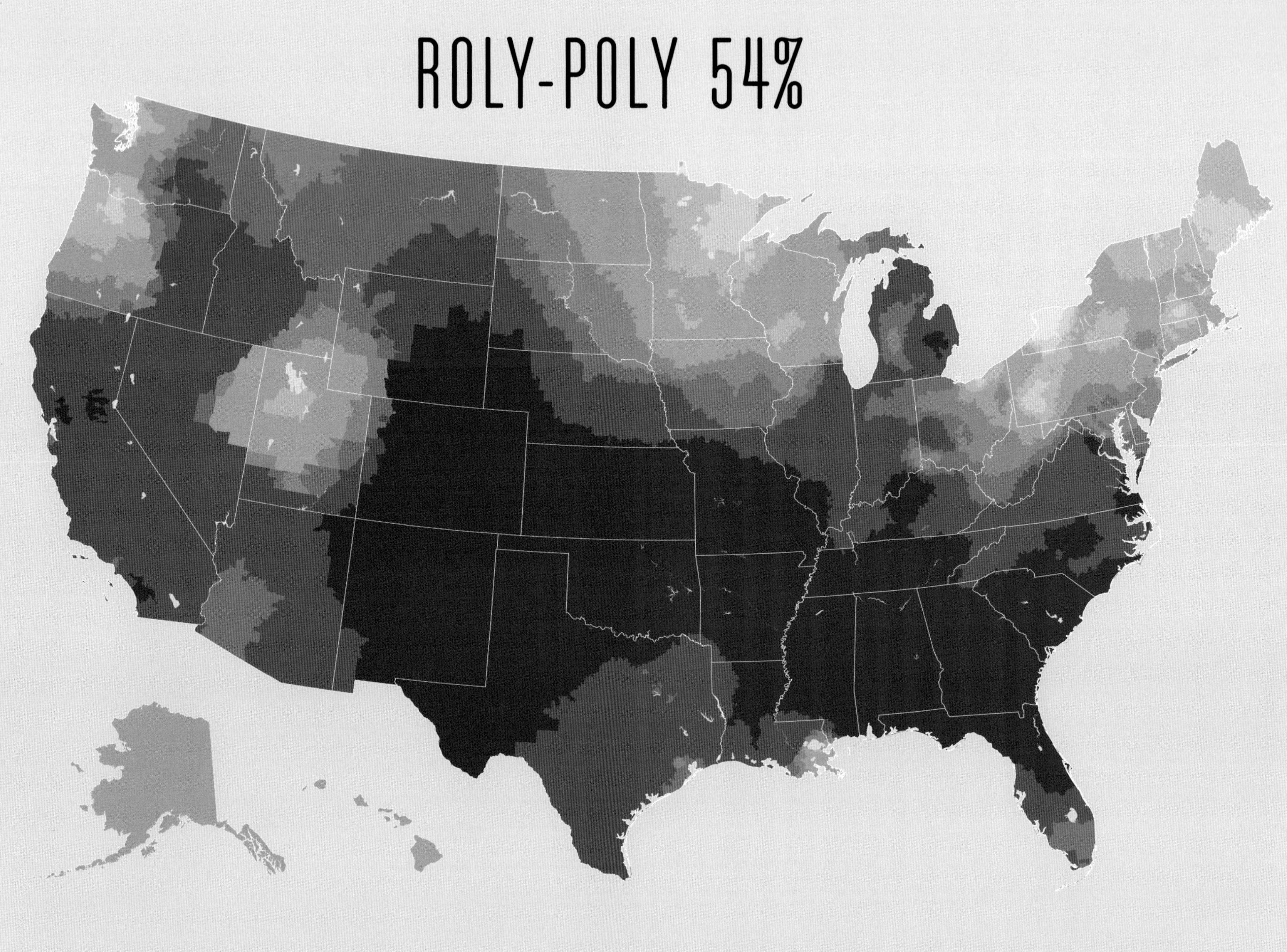
ROLY-POLY 54%
PERCENT SAYING
0
10
20
30
40
50
75%

PILLBUG 13%

POTATO BUG 10%

CENTIPEDE 3%

NO WORD FOR THIS 11%

DOODLEBUG 3%

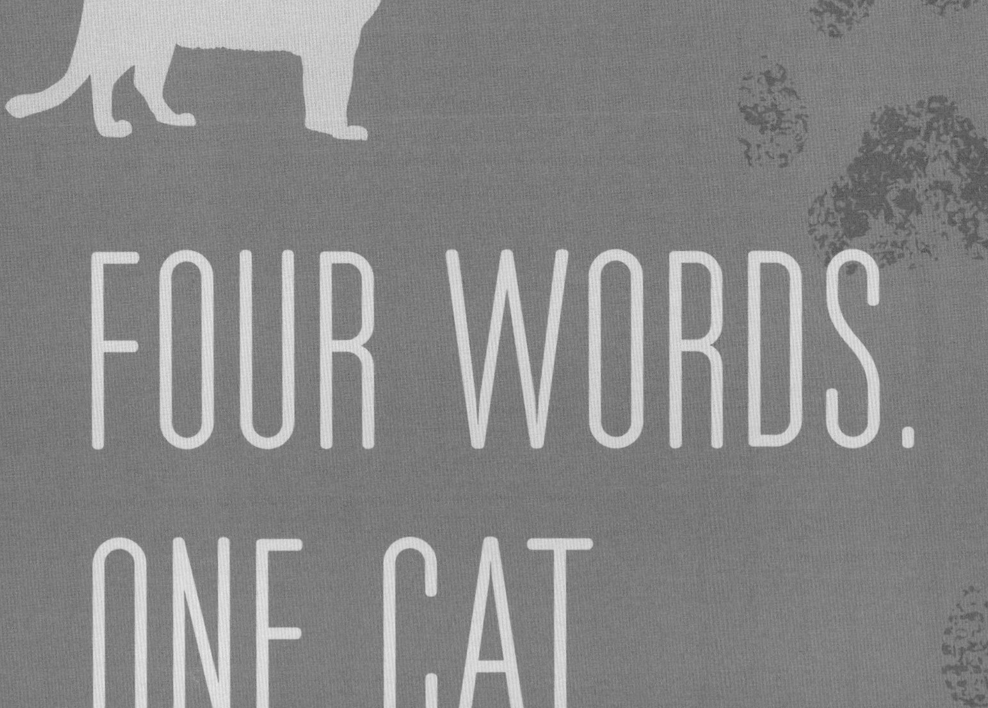
FOUR WORDS.
ONE CAT.

You may have heard people talk about *mountain lions, cougars, catamounts,* and *panthers* without realizing that they're talking about the same animal.

Panther is distinctly Floridian. It is one of the few quirks of both the northern and southern Florida dialects, and its use falls sharply at the state line. Within Florida, usage tops 40 percent, but Mobile, Alabama, just west of the Florida Panhandle, is the only place outside the state where more than 10 percent of people use the word.

The rarest name of the four is *catamount*. It's not the most common term anywhere in the country, but it reaches its peak popularity around Burlington, Vermont, where more than 20 percent of people choose the word. The high for every region outside of Vermont is 3 percent. No wonder the University of Vermont, which is in Burlington, calls its teams the Catamounts.

While *panther* and *cougar* are two of the more common team nicknames in sports, *catamount* has yet to catch on to the same extent. The only other *catamounts* I could find are at Western Carolina University, in Cullowhee, North Carolina.

MOUNTAIN LION 75%

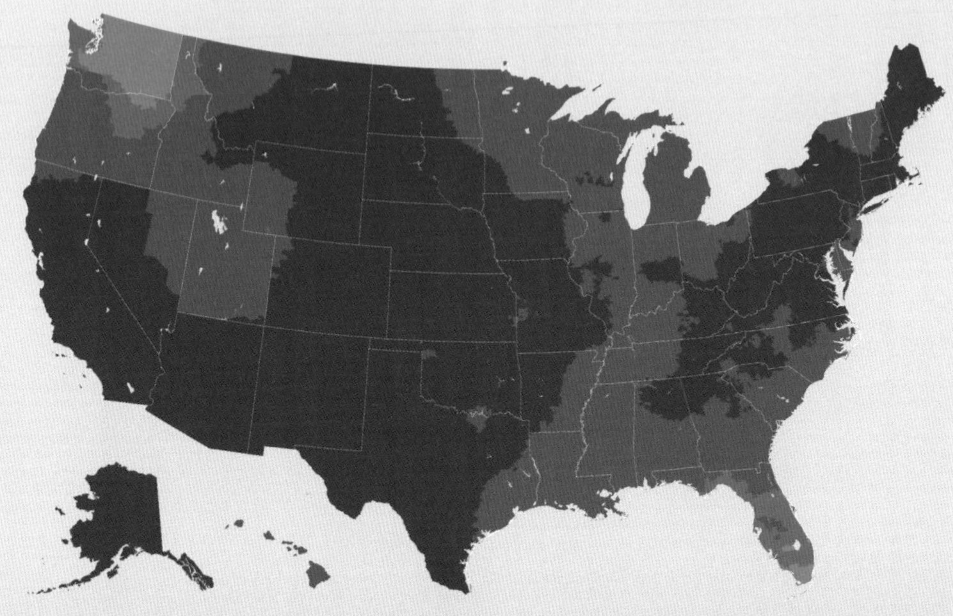

COUGAR 18%

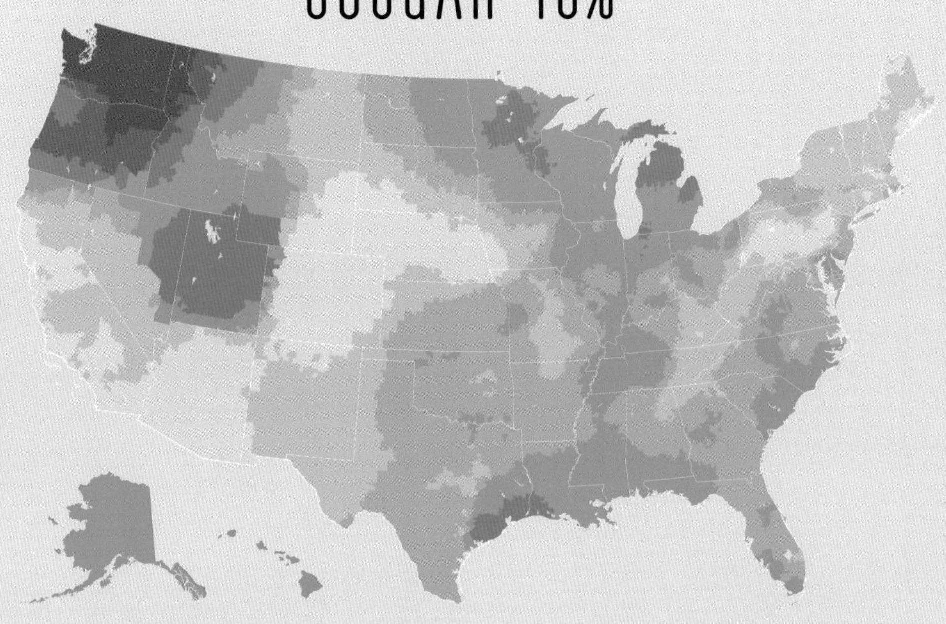

PERCENT SAYING

0 10 20 30 40 50 75%

CATAMOUNT <1%

PANTHER 4%

WHAT WE CALL IT WHEN

IT'S RAINING WHILE THE SUN IS SHINING

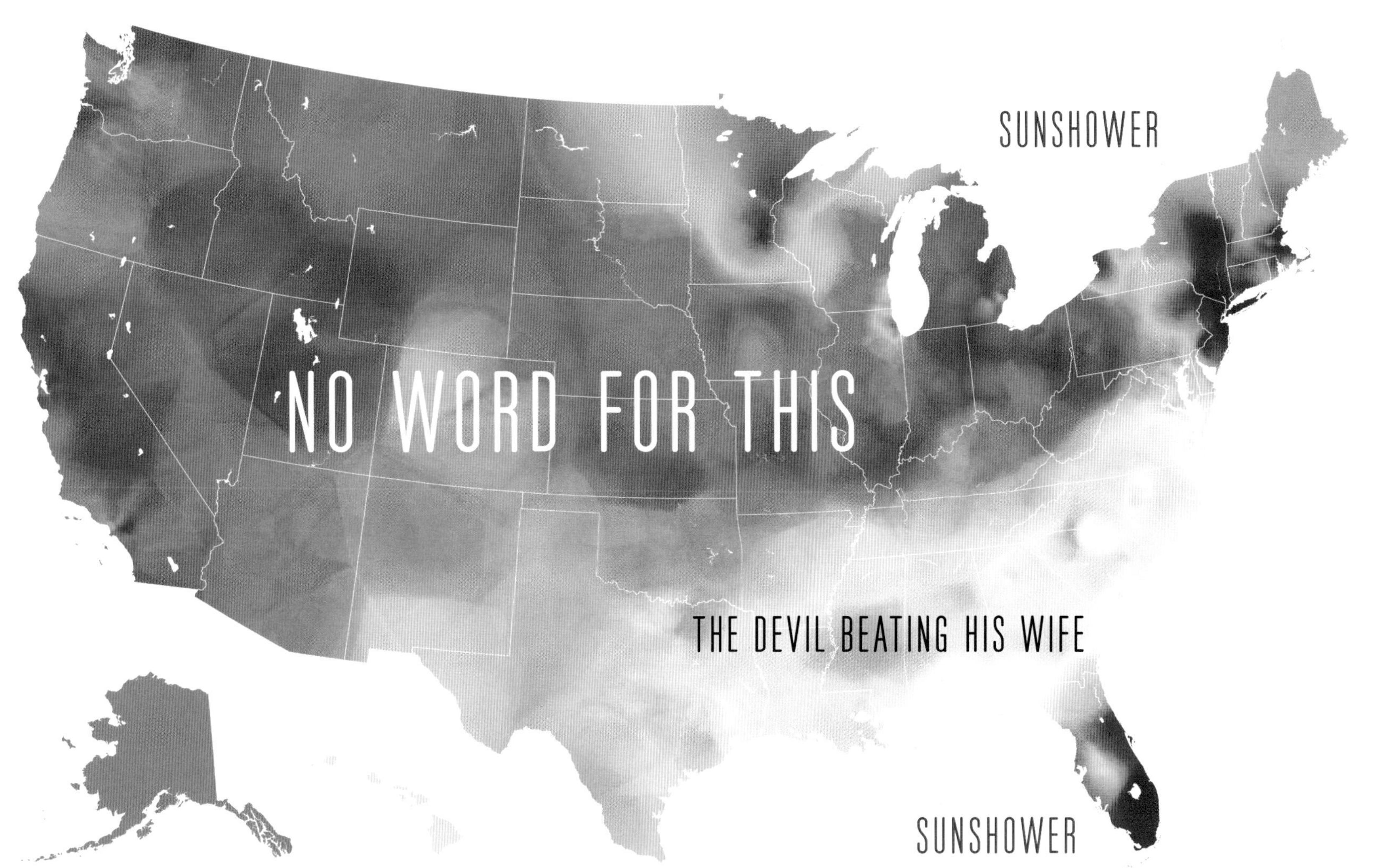
SUNSHOWER
NO WORD FOR THIS
THE DEVIL BEATING HIS WIFE
SUNSHOWER

THE DEVIL BEATING HIS WIFE

I'm a northerner, and nothing surprised me more in my research than the evocative phrase *the devil beating his wife* for the mixture of sun and rain that I've known all my life as a *sunshower.*

The mix of sun and rain is sufficiently odd that it brings out folk expressions in a staggering number of languages. Many involve the wedding or birth of various animals—*fox's wedding* (Japanese), *the wolf is having a baby* (Armenian), *the leopard is giving birth* (Luganda), or *a wedding for monkeys* (Zulu). References to *the devil beating his wife* are found in Dutch and Hungarian. In Bulgarian and Turkish, *the devil is getting married*.

Jonathon Green, author of the authoritative *Green's Dictionary of Slang,* traces the expression back to the French idiom *le diable bat sa femme et marie sa fille* (the devil beats his wife and marries his daughter), an expression that has been reported to have taken hold in the south of France.

Regardless of its provenance, the phrase is still widely used in the Deep South. Over half of respondents in and around Mississippi and Alabama use it.

In **HAWAII**, the same phenomenon is often known as *liquid sun*.

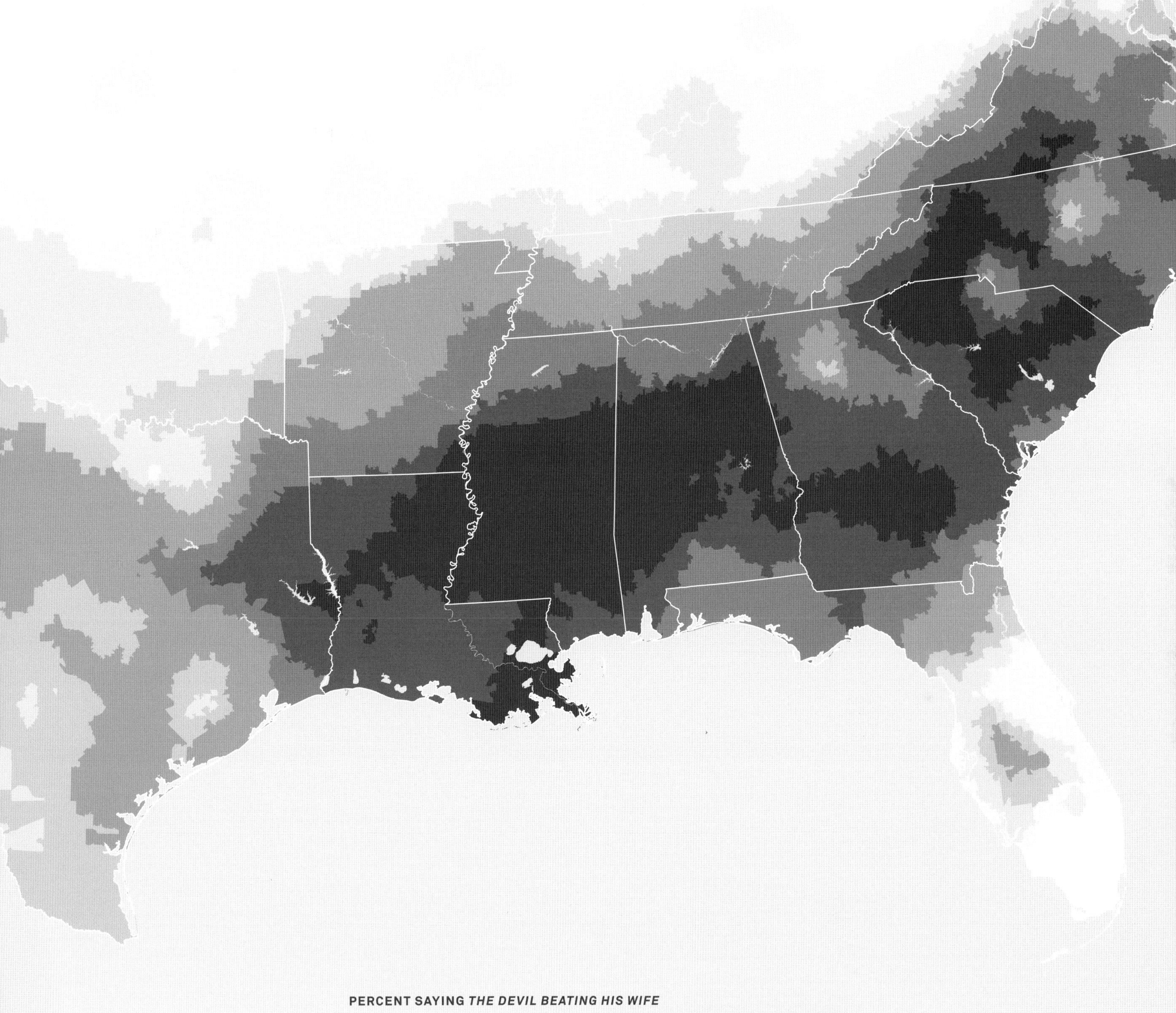

PERCENT SAYING *THE DEVIL BEATING HIS WIFE*

0 10 20 30 40 >50%

HOW TO PRETEND YOU'RE FROM

MISSOURI

Missouri is divided culturally between Kansas City in the west and St. Louis in the east. And it isn't only a difference in barbecue styles or baseball-team affections that signal you've crossed the dividing line.

The strongest linguistic dividing line is our good friend *cot* vs. *caught*. In St. Louis, the vowels are still distinct among almost 90 percent of the population. In Kansas City, less than 25 percent of residents still pronounce *cot* differently than *caught*. The two metro areas have been different in this respect for some time. But while Kansas City used to be the outlier, St. Louis now is. It's the only place in the region where the unmerged outnumber the merged.

One of St. Louis's other strongest distinctions, relative to the rest of the region, is the persistence of *soda*. *Pop* territory lies to the north in Iowa and to the west in Kansas, and Arkansas and Tennessee are *coke* country. Start traveling farther east, into Indiana, and you're also likely to hear more people say something other than *soda* (*coke* in Evansville, *pop* in Fort Wayne). But not so in St. Louis, where 93 percent of people say *soda*—the second-highest concentration anywhere outside the Northeast. Milwaukee is at 94 percent.

The last St. Louis tick is Missouri's word for the small roads that run parallel to highways. What do you call them? If you say *frontage roads,* there's about an 80 percent chance that you're from the Kansas City portion of the state instead of the St. Louis portion, where it's more likely that you say *service roads* or *outer roads*.

If you find yourself in a room full of Missourians and want to figure out whether you're talking to someone from Kansas City or St. Louis—without being so forward as to ask—just watch for whether they

- say *soda,*
- don't call those small roads *frontage roads,* and
- pronounce *cot* and *caught* differently.

If they meet all three criteria, there's a 95 percent chance you're talking to someone from St. Louis.

HOW TO PRETEND YOU'RE FROM

OKLAHOMA

Head on down to the *beer barn* and bring the brews back to your house in a *sack*. In Oklahoma the first syllable of *lawyer* sounds like *law* and the last syllable of *Texas* sounds like it's spelled with a *z*. Use a *tea towel* to dry your dishes, and head down to the *creek* to catch some *crawdads*. This speech region bleeds over into the Texas Panhandle to the west and parts of Arkansas to the east.

HOW TO PRETEND YOU'RE FROM

KENTUCKY

Where *crayon* sounds like *krown*, highways are *expressways*, and *you all* might order a *soft drink* or a *coke* with your *carry-out*. Try some *Kentucky oysters* (chitterlings, pronounced *chit-lins*), if you have the stomach for them (they're made from the small intestines of freshly slaughtered pigs). If not, perhaps stick with the *Kentucky jam cake* instead—a layer cake with jam blended into the batter, often served with caramel *icing* (not *frosting*).

CONCLUSION

Language is a fundamental part of the human experience. The words we use to describe our lives become indelible marks of our identity, of who we are and where we come from.

And if American English says anything about us, it's that we have many identities, are many different peoples, and come from all over. Something as simple as whether you say *soda* or *pop*, *hoagie* or *sub*, *you guys* or *y'all*—these distinctions help form the cornerstones of people's identity. They are reminders of our personal histories and our families.

In this book, we have seen how *traffic circles* became *roundabouts,* charted the exact boundary line where *semi-trucks* turn into *tractor-trailers,* and explored the origins of and meanings behind everything from *lightning bugs* to *stoops* to *shopping carts*.

Dialect variation in American English shows no sign of disappearing, even as other parts of culture become less local and more national. No matter how much media we consume, we inevitably acquire the speech patterns of the people we surround ourselves with. Our parents, our siblings, and our childhood friends have an impact that far outweighs any homogenizing effects of television, film, or the Internet. The words we use will continue to reveal the contours of our cultural geography, as each ensuing generation redefines what it means to speak American.

INDEX OF TERMS USED

M

N

O

P

Q

R

S

T

V

W

Y

Z

INDEX OF PLACES